Praise for *Things I Don't Want to Know*

"Deborah Levy's rich response to George Orwell's famous 1946 essay 'Why I Write' is unmissable . . . Like Orwell, Levy is entertaining and makes his categories her chapter headings. But, unlike Orwell, she is not steadily organized. She is a maker not a clearer up of mysteries . . . It is this that gives the book its subtle, unpredictable, surprising atmosphere."

— *The Guardian*

"Here, writing is a way of dealing with the experiences of injustice and despair, and perhaps with the underlying realisation that as an author, one often ends up being drawn towards such sadness— the only way to process the 'knowledge that we cannot bear to live with,' by trying to render it itself something useful or beautiful, or both. Even if Levy does not draw any categorical principles in the manner of Orwell, this sensitive conclusion ought to resonate with any writers who care to remember how they became socially aware."

— *New Statesman*

THINGS I DON'T
WANT TO KNOW

BY THE SAME AUTHOR

Fiction
Black Vodka (stories)
Swimming Home
Pillow Talk in Europe and Other Places (stories)
Billy and Girl
The Unloved
Swallowing Geography
Beautiful Mutants
Ophelia and the Great Idea

Poetry
An Amorous Discourse in the Suburbs of Hell

Plays
Pax
Heresies
Clam
Call Blue Jane
Shiny Nylon
The B File: An Erotic Interrogation
of Five Female Personas
Pushing the Price into Denmark
Honey Baby Middle England
Macbeth—False Memories

Deborah Levy

—

THINGS I DON'T
WANT TO KNOW

—

On Writing

B L O O M S B U R Y

NEW YORK • LONDON • NEW DELHI • SYDNEY

Published by Bloomsbury USA, New York
Bloomsbury is a trademark of Bloomsbury Publishing Plc

All papers used by Bloomsbury USA are natural,
recyclable products made from wood grown in
well-managed forests. The manufacturing processes
conform to the environmental regulations of
the country of origin.

LIBRARY OF CONGRESS CATALOGING-IN-PUBLICATION DATA
HAS BEEN APPLIED FOR

ISBN: 978-1-62040-565-9

First published in Great Britain in 2013 by Notting Hill Editions Ltd
First U.S. Edition 2014

1 3 5 7 9 10 8 6 4 2

Designed by FLOK Design, Berlin, Germany
Typeset by CB editions, London
Printed and bound in the U.S.A. by Thomson-
Shore Inc., Dexter, Michigan

Bloomsbury books may be purchased for business or
promotional use. For information on bulk purchases
please contact Macmillan Corporate and Premium Sales
Department at specialmarkets@macmillan.com.

All animals are equal but some animals are more equal
than others.
– George Orwell, *Animal Farm* (1945)

I know roughly speaking, how I became a writer. I don't
know precisely why. In order to exist, did I really need to
line up words and sentences? In order to exist, was it enough
for me to be the author of a few books? . . . One day I shall
certainly have to start using words to uncover what is real,
to uncover my reality.
– Georges Perec, *Species of Spaces and other Pieces* (1974)

THINGS I DON'T
WANT TO KNOW

One

– Political Purpose –

You are – your life, and nothing else.
Jean-Paul Sartre, *No Exit* (1944)

T hat spring when life was very hard and I was at war with my lot and simply couldn't see where there was to get to, I seemed to cry most on escalators at train stations. Going down them was fine but there was something about standing still and being carried upwards that did it. From apparently nowhere tears poured out of me and by the time I got to the top and felt the wind rushing in, it took all my effort to stop myself from sobbing. It was as if the momentum of the escalator carrying me forwards and upwards was a physical expression of a conversation I was having with myself. Escalators, which in the early days of their invention were known as 'travelling staircases' or 'magic stairways', had mysteriously become danger zones.

I made sure I had lots to read on train journeys. This was the first time in my life I had ever been pleased to read newspaper columns about the things that happened to the journalist's lawnmower. When I wasn't absorbed in this kind of thing (which I experienced as being shot with a tranquilliser dart) the book I read most was Gabriel Garcia Marquez's short novel, *Of Love and Other Demons*. Out of all the loved and loveless characters dreaming and scheming in hammocks under the blue Caribbean sky, the only one that really interested me was Bernarda Cabrera, the dissolute wife of a Marquis who has given up on life and his marriage. To escape from her own life Bernarda Cabrera is introduced to 'magic chocolate' from Oaxaca by her slave lover and starts to live in a state of delirium. Addicted to sacks of cacao and fermented honey, she spends most of the day lying naked on her bedroom floor, 'enveloped in the glow of her lethal gases'. By the time I got off the train and started to weep on the escalator that apparently was inviting me to read my mind (at a time in my life I preferred to read other things) I began to regard Bernarda as a role model.

I knew things had to change when one week I found myself staring intently at a poster in my bathroom titled 'The Skeletal System'. This featured a human skeleton with its inner organs and bones labelled in Latin and which I constantly misread as 'The Societal System'. I made a decision. If escalators had become machines with torrid emotionality, a system that transported me to places I did not want to go, why not book a flight to somewhere I actually did want to go?

Three days later, I zipped up my brand new

laptop and found myself sitting in aisle seat 22C heading for Palma, Majorca. As the plane took off I realised that being stranded between the earth and the sky was a bit like being on an escalator. The man unlucky enough to be sitting next to a weeping woman looked like he had once been in the army and now spent his life lying on a beach. I was pleased my cheap airline buddy was a tough guy with hard square shoulders and jagged welts of sunburn striping his thick neck but I did not want anyone to attempt to comfort me. If anything my tears seemed to send him into a tantric shopping coma because he called for the air hostess and ordered two cans of beer, a vodka and coke, an extra coke, a tube of Pringles, a scratchcard, a teddy bear stuffed with mini chocolate bars, a Swiss watch on special offer, and asked the crew if the airline had one of those questionnaires to fill in where you get a free holiday if it's drawn out of the hat. The tanned military man pushed the teddy bear into my face and said, 'That'll cheer you up if nothing will,' as if the bear was a handkerchief with glass eyes sewn on it.

When the plane landed in Palma at 11p.m., the only taxi driver prepared to drive me up the steep mountain roads might have been blind because he had white clouds floating across both his eyes. No one in the queue wanted to admit they were anxious he would crash the car and avoided him when he pulled up at the taxi rank. After we negotiated the price, he managed to drive without looking at the road and instead had his fingers on the dial of the radio while staring at his feet. An hour later he began to manoeuvre his Mercedes up a narrow road lined with pine trees that I knew went on for a deceptively long time. He managed to get half way up and then suddenly shouted NO NO NO and abruptly stopped the car. For the first time all spring I wanted to laugh. We both sat in the dark, a rabbit running through the grass, neither of us knowing what to do next. In the end I gave him a generous tip for driving so dangerously and started the long walk up the dark path that I vaguely remembered led to the hotel.

The smell of wood fires in the stone houses below and the bells on sheep grazing in the mountains and the strange silence that happens in between the bells chiming suddenly made me want to smoke. I had long given up smoking but at the airport I had bought a packet of Spanish cigarettes, fully intending to start again. I sat down on a damp rock under a tree that was a little way off the path, pushed my laptop between my shins and lit up under the stars.

Smoking cheap Spanish filthy sock-tobacco under a pine tree was so much better than trying to hold it together on escalators. There was something comforting about being literally lost when I was lost in every other way and just as I was thinking I might have to sleep on the mountain that night, I heard someone shout my name. A number of things happened at once. I heard the sound of someone on the path and then I saw the feet of a woman in red leather shoes making her way towards me. She shouted my name again but for some reason I was unable to attach the name she was shouting to myself. Suddenly a torch was being shone in my face and when she saw me sitting on a rock under a tree smoking a cigarette, the woman said, 'Ah there you are.'

The woman's face was shockingly pale and I wondered if she was mad. But then I remembered I was the mad one because she was trying to get me off my rock on the edge of a mountain dressed for the beach on a night when the temperature had fallen to below freezing.

'I saw you walking in to the forest. I think you are lost eh?'

I nodded, but must have looked confused because she said, 'I am Maria.'

Maria was the owner of the hotel and she looked much older and sadder than the last time we met. She probably thought the same about me.

'Hello Maria.'

I stood up. 'Thank you for coming to find me.'

We walked in silence back to the hotel and she pointed with her torch to the turning where I had missed the path, as if she was a detective gathering evidence for something neither of us could fathom.

People who book into this *pensión* want particular things: a quiet place near the citrus orchards and

5

waterfalls, cheap large rooms, a calm place to rest and think. There is no mini bar or TV, no hot water, no room service. Never advertised in tourist guides, word of mouth alone made sure it was always full in season. The first time I stayed here was in my early twenties when I was writing my first novel on a Smith Corona typewriter which I carried in a pillow case; then in my late thirties when I was in love and carrying what was then called a 'luggable' computer. I had to buy a special bag for it, a long rectangle with extra padding and little compartments for the mouse and keyboard. I was very proud of it and even prouder of being able to set it up in any hotel room with the extension lead I had bought at the airport. The parched August afternoon I lugged my luggable (very heavy) computer up this mountain, plus all my other bags, I was wearing a short blue cotton dress and suede walking shoes and was as happy as it is possible to be. When happiness is happening it feels as if nothing else happened before it, it is a sensation that happens only in the present tense. I liked being on my own with the knowledge that I was returning to my sweetheart, the great love of my life. I phoned him every evening from the old fashioned call box next to the pizzeria, holding on tight to the fistful of sweaty 100 peseta coins that connected us to each other's voice, rolling the coins in to the slot, believing that love, Great Love, was the only season I would ever live in.

If love had changed to something else, something I did not recognise, the terrace at the front of the *pensión* with its tables and chairs placed under the olive trees looked exactly the same as it did when I last stayed here. Everything was the same. The ornate tiled floor. The heavy wooden doors that opened out onto the ancient palm tree in the courtyard. The polished grand piano that stood majestically in the hallway. The thick cold stone of the whitewashed walls. My room was exactly the same too, except this time when I opened the doors of the worm eaten wardrobe and saw the same four bent wire clothes hangers on the rail, they seemed to mimic the shape of forlorn human shoulders.

I started to perform the familiar rituals of travelling alone, as I had done so often in my life; untangling wires and precariously plugging in the European adapter with two pins, switching on my computer, charging up my mobile, arranging on the small writing desk the two books and one notebook I had brought with me. First of all the well thumbed *Of Love and Other Demons*, and secondly, George Sand's *A Winter in Majorca*, an account of the year she spent in Majorca with her lover, Frederick Chopin, and her two children from her first marriage. The notebook I had brought with me was labelled 'POLAND, 1988'. It would probably be more romantic to describe it as 'my journal', or 'my diary', but I thought of it as a note book, perhaps even a sheriff's notebook because I was always gathering evidence for something I could not fathom.

In 1988 I was taking notes in Poland, but what for? I found myself flicking through its pages to remind myself.

In October 1988 I had been invited to write about a performance directed by the renowned Polish actress, Zofia Kalinska, who had collaborated on many productions with the theatre director, painter and auteur, Tandeusz Kantor. My notebook starts at Heathrow, London. I am on a plane (LOT airlines) heading for Warsaw. Nearly all the passengers are chain smoking and the entire female cabin crew have dyed their hair platinum blonde. When they wheel the trolley down the aisle to deliver an unidentifiable 'soft drink' (cherry juice?) in a grey plastic cup to the enthusiastic smokers, they resemble belligerent nurses delivering medication to their troublesome patients. This scene turned up in a novel I wrote two decades later – the cabin crew on LOT airlines become nurses who have been imported from Lithuania, Odessa and Kiev to deliver electroshock therapy to patients in a hospital in Kent, England.

This novel, it seems, is what I had been gathering evidence for, twenty years before actually writing it.

And then my notebook tells me I am on a train in Warsaw, wagon 5, seat 71, heading for Krakow where Zofia Kalinska is based. Here I witness a scene that would not be out of place in one of Kantor's performances. A soldier is saying goodbye to three women – his sister, his mother and his girlfriend. First he kisses his mother's hand. Then he kisses his sister's cheek. Finally he kisses his girlfriend's lips. I also note that Poland's economy is collapsing, that the government has increased food prices by 40 per cent, that there have been strikes and demonstrations at the iron and steel works in Nowa Huta and the Gdansk ship yard.

It seems that what interests me (in my sheriff's notebook) is the act of kissing in the middle of a political catastrophe.

I am in Krakow. Zofia Kalinska wears two (shamanistic) necklaces to the rehearsal of her play: one made from cloudy turquoise and one from wormwood. I note that absinthe is made from wormwood. Didn't the ancient Egyptians soak wormwood in wine and use it as a remedy for various afflictions? I had read somewhere that absinthe, with its heady mix of fennel and green anise was given to the French troops in the early nineteenth century to prevent malaria. The soldiers returned to France with a taste for the 'green fairy'. If they were not bitten by mosquitoes, they had nevertheless been nipped by a winged creature, a metaphor, as they lay wounded and hallucinating on their camp beds. I remind myself to ask Zofia about her necklaces. She is in her early sixties and has performed in some of the most famous avant-garde theatre productions in Europe – including Kantor's *Dead Class*, in which a number of apparently dead characters are confronted by mannequins who remind them of their youthful dreams. Today, Zofia has a few notes to give to her Western European actors.

'The form must never be bigger than the content, especially in Poland. This is to do with our history: suppression, the Germans, the Russians, we feel ashamed because we have so much emotion. We must use emotion carefully in the theatre, we must not imitate emotion. In my productions, which have been described as "surreal", there is no such thing as a surreal emotion. At the same time, we are not making psychological theatre, we are not imitating reality.'

She tells a young actress to speak up.

'To speak up is not about speaking louder, it is about feeling entitled to voice a wish. We always hesitate when we wish for something. In my theatre, I like to show the hesitation and not to conceal it. A hesitation is not the same as a pause. It is an attempt to defeat the wish. But when you are ready to catch this wish and put it in to language, then you can whisper but the audience will always hear you.'

And then she has an idea. She says the costume for the actress playing Medea is all wrong. Medea murdered her children so she should wear a dress with a hole cut out of its stomach. Zofia explains that this is a poetic image, but the actress must not speak her lines like poetry.

It occurred to me that I had jogged along with Zofia's notes to her actors in my own writing for much of my life. Content should be bigger than form – yes, that was a subversive note to a writer like myself who had always experimented with form, but it is the wrong note for a writer who has never experimented with form. And it is the wrong note for a writer who has never wondered what would happen if the Warsaw soldier kissed his mother on her lips and his girlfriend on her hand. And yes, there was no such thing as a surreal emotion. Her other message was that emotion, which always terrifies the avant-garde's stiff upper lip, is better conveyed in a voice that is like ice. As for the strategies a writer of fiction might employ to unfold the ways in which her characters attempt to defeat a long held wish – for myself it is the story of this hesitation that is the point of writing.

I did not know why I had bought the Polish notebook with me to Majorca. Actually I did know. Scribbled on the back of the cover were two Polish menus that I had asked Zofia to translate into English for me:

White borscht with boiled egg and sausage.
Traditional hunter's stew with mash potatoes.
Soft drink.

Traditional Polish cucumber soup.
Cabbage leaves stuffed with meat and mash
potatoes. Soft drink.

I had used these same menus in the as-yet un-published novel *Swimming Home* I had written two decades later, the novel in which the cabin crew on LOT airlines had morphed into nurses from Odessa, but I did not want to think about this. I closed the notebook. After a while I placed it on the small writing desk and then I rearranged the chair.

The next morning, when I woke up at 8am I could hear Maria shouting at her brother who was shouting at the cleaner. I had forgotten how every-one shouts in Southern Europe and how doors bang and dogs bark all the time and from the valley there is always the sound of more banging from the build-ing of stone walls, the mending of sheds and chicken coops and fences.

And another sound. Something so eerily famil-iar, I wanted to put my fingers in my ears. As I made my way down to the terrace for breakfast, I heard a woman sobbing. HUH HUH HUH. I did not want to hear that some of the HUHs were longer than others and that these carried the most sorrow for the length of the breath. The sobbing came from the utility room just above the terrace where the brooms and mops were kept. Maria was weeping into her arms that were resting on top of the washing machine. She saw me make my way to a table and turned her back on me.

Ten minutes later she brought out breakfast on a silver tray: small bowls of home-made yogurt and dark honey, warm bread rolls , a large cup of aromatic coffee with a jug of milk on the side, a glass of spring water with a slice of lemon in it, and two fresh apricots. As she unloaded the tray, Maria never once asked me about my life in London or I about hers in Majorca. I made sure I barely looked at her but I reckoned I was a detective gathering evidence for something neither of us could fathom.

Maria was one of the few women in this Catholic village who had neither married or had children. Perhaps she was wary of these rituals because she knew they would ultimately exploit her. Whatever, it was clear that she had other kinds of projects in mind. She had designed the irrigation system that watered the citrus orchard, and of course, the ambience of this inexpensive, tranquil hotel was designed by her too. If it mostly attracted solo travellers, it was possible that Maria had quietly and slyly constructed a place that was a refuge from The Family. A place that was also her home (her brother lived elsewhere with his wife) but a home she did not entirely own – all financial arrangements were handled by her brother. All the same, Maria had made a bid for a life that did not include the rituals of marriage and motherhood.

As I bit into the sweet orange flesh of the apricot, I found myself thinking about some of the women, the mothers who had waited with me in the school playground while we collected our children. Now that we were mothers we were all shadows of our former selves, chased by the women we used to be before we had children. We didn't really know what to do with her, this fierce, independent young woman who followed us about, shouting and pointing the finger while we wheeled our buggies in the English rain. We tried to answer her back but we did not have the language to explain that we were not women who had merely 'acquired' some children – we had metamorphosed (new heavy bodies, milk in our breasts, hormonally-programmed to run to our babies when they cried) in to someone we did not entirely understand.

Feminine fertility and pregnancy not only continue to fascinate our collective imagination, but also serve as a sanctuary for the sacred . . . Today motherhood is imbued with what has survived of *religious feeling*.

– Julia Kristeva, *Motherhood Today* (2005)

Mother was The Woman the whole world had imagined to death. It proved very hard to re-negotiate the world's nostalgic phantasy about our purpose in life. The trouble was that we too had all sorts of wild imaginings about what Mother should 'be' and were cursed with the desire to not be disappointing. We did not yet entirely understand that Mother, as imagined and politicised by the societal system, was a delusion. The world loved the delusion more than it loved the mother. All the same, we felt guilty about unveiling this delusion in case the niche we had made for ourselves and our much-loved children collapsed in ruins around our muddy trainers – which were probably sewn together by child slaves in sweatshops all over the globe. It was mysterious because it seemed to me that the male world and its political arrangements (never in favour of children and women) was actually jealous of the passion we felt for our babies. Like everything that involves love, our children made us happy beyond measure – and unhappy too – but never as miserable as the twenty-first century Neo-Patriarchy made us feel. It required us to be passive but ambitious, maternal but erotically energetic, self-sacrificing but fulfilled – we were to be Strong Modern Women whilst being subjected to all kinds of humiliations, both economic and domestic. If we felt guilty about everything most of the time, we were not sure what it was we had actually done wrong.

Something strange had happened to the way a particular group of the women I met in the school playground used language. They said words that were childlike but not as interesting as the words children made up. Words like groany moany smiley

fabby cheery veggie sniffy. And they made an uneasy distance between themselves and the working
class mothers they called chavs. The chavs in the
playground had less money and less education and
ate more chocolate and crisps and other nice things.
They said words like, Oh my God, I didn't know
where to look. In the balance I thought these were
the more exciting words.

Oh My God

I did not know where to look

If the Oh My Gods were channelling William
Blake, the language that came out of the mouths
of the smiley sniffy groany cheery women was not
so much grown up as grown down. I listened to all
those mothers in a daze because I knew we were all
exhausted and making the best of our new niche in
the Societal System. This fact made us all a bit odd
in my view.

Adrienne Rich, who I was reading at the time,
said it exactly like it is: 'No woman is really an insider
in the institutions fathered by masculine consciousness.' That was the weird thing. It was becoming
clear to me that Motherhood was an institution fathered by masculine consciousness. This male consciousness was male unconsciousness. It needed its
female partners who were also mothers to stamp on
her own desires and attend to his desires, and then
to everyone else's desires. We had a go at cancelling
our own desires and found we had a talent for it.

And we put a lot of our life's energy into creating a home for our children and for our men.

A house means a family house, a place specially meant for putting children and men in so as to restrict their waywardness and distract them from the longing for adventure and escape they've had since time began. The most difficult thing in tackling this subject is to get down to the basic and utterly manageable terms in which women see the fantastic challenge a house represents: how to provide a centre for children and men at the same time . . . The house a woman creates is a Utopia. She can't help it – can't help trying to interest her nearest and dearest not in happiness itself but in the search for it.

    – Marguerite Duras, *Practicalities* (1987)

There is no one who said it more ruthlessly, or kindly, than Marguerite Duras. There is no feminist critical theory or philosophy I have read that cuts deeper. Marguerite wore massive spectacles and she had a massive ego. Her massive ego helped her crush delusions about femininity under each of her shoes – which were smaller than her spectacles. When she wasn't too drunk she found the intellectual energy to move on and crush another one. Perhaps when Orwell described sheer egoism as a necessary quality for a writer, he was not thinking about the sheer egoism of a female writer. Even the most arrogant female writer has to work over time to build an ego that is robust enough to get her through January, never mind all the way to December. I hear Duras's hard-earned ego speaking to me, to me, to me, in all the seasons.

Men and women are different, after all. Being a mother isn't the same as being a father. Motherhood means that a woman gives her body over to her child, her children; they're on her as they might be on a hill, in a garden; they devour her, hit her, sleep on her; and she lets herself be devoured, and sometimes she sleeps because they are on her body. Nothing like that happens with fathers.

But perhaps women secrete their own despair in the process of being mothers and wives. Perhaps, their whole lives long, they lose their rightful kingdom in the despair of every day. Perhaps their youthful aspirations, their strength, their love, all leak away through wounds given and received completely legally. Perhaps that's what it is – that women and martyrdom go together. And that women who are completely fulfilled by showing off their competence, their skill at games, their cooking and their virtue are two-a-penny.

– Marguerite Duras, *Practicalities* (1987)

Was Marguerite Duras suggesting that women are not so much a dark continent as a well-lit suburb? If maternity is the only female signifier, we know that the baby on our lap, if it is healthy and well cared for, will eventually turn away from our breast and see someone else. He will see an other. He will see the world and he will fall in love with it. Some mothers go mad because the world that made them feel worthless is the same world with which their children fall in love. The suburb of femininity is not a good place to live. Nor is it wise to seek refuge inside our children because children are always keen to make their way in to the world to meet someone else. Yes, there had been many times I called my daughters back to zip up their coats. All the same, I knew they would rather be cold and free.

It was said that I refused to grant any value to the maternal instinct and to love. This was not so. I simply asked that women should experience them truthfully and freely, whereas they often use them as excuses and take refuge in them, only to find themselves imprisoned in that refuge when those emotions have dried up in their hearts.

    – Simone de Beauvoir, *Force of Circumstances*,
      Vol. III (1963)

I began to see the groanies and moanies in the playground as human skeletons wearing pastel cardigans with sequins sewn on to the buttons. The Oh my Gods were skeletons wearing tracksuits. We were all uneasy in the Societal System that divided the playground so forensically and stupidly into rich and poor skeletons.

A particular mother of my acquaintance had eyes so small the moanies and groanies would have called them piggy eyes. It was not that her eyes were literally small, it was as if they wanted to disappear in to her head. Every time we met in the playground, I found myself trying not to stare but I couldn't help myself. When her tiny peepholes tried to wriggle away from my gaze, it was usually when she was insisting (unusually, it has to be said) that her charismatic but bullying husband was the love of her life. In fact he had loved her right out of her life. I remember thinking at the time, yes, never mistake hate for love.

It was as if she had told herself in the voice of the masculine consciousness she imitated, but had no rights to inhabit, that she did not suffer fools gladly (me) and that she stood for certain kinds of values. Most confusing of all, she was required to raise the children more or less without her husband's participation, yet feel entitled on his behalf to mock and judge the single mothers on the other side of the playground. The way she ventriloquised her husband's values and standards sounded not so much crazy, as crazed. She was really not very likeable but I began to regard her as a political prisoner. It seemed to me that her eyes wanted to disappear into her head because she did not want to see that the reality she had bought into might just slaughter her.

And what about my own eyes? My eyes which so quickly filled with tears on escalators were trying not to stare at all that was wrong in my own situation, but, Oh my God, they didn't know where to look.

I was certainly not looking at Maria who was now sweeping the courtyard with her back turned to me.

I decided to visit the village shop to look for the

pure chocolate that had so intoxicated Marquez's errant fictional wife, Bernarda Cabrera. The strange thing was I found it. There in front of me, lying with the other bars of more familiar confectionery, was a bar of CHOCOLATE NEGRO EXTRAFINO: CACAO 99%. Ingredientes: cacao, azucar. It even had a warning on the wrapper telling me this chocolate was 'intensidad'. The owner of the grocery store was a distinguished Chinese man originally from Shanghai. For as long as I had known him he was always reading books behind the counter, tortoise-shell spectacles perched half-way down his nose. His black hair was now streaked with silver as we exchanged superficial greetings: how are you, yes not many tourists at this time of year, yes it is very cold, the forecast said it might even snow, how was I going to spend my day?

I told him I was about to walk to the next village to see the monastery where George Sand and Frederick Chopin stayed during the winter of 1838.

He smiled but it was a more of a grimace. Ah yes. Jorge Sand. The Majorcans did not like her. She dressed in men's clothing and she said Majorcans preferred their pigs to people. No. Jorge Sand was not a woman he would like to share a bottle of wine with. When I laughed I was not really sure what I was laughing about or who I was laughing at. I paid him for the chocolate, and then as a second thought bought an extra bar of the 99% cacao for Maria.

George Sand (who was really Baroness Amantine Aurore Lucile Dupin) smoked large cigars to get through her day. She would have needed them living in the gloomy Carthusian monastery of Jesus the Nazare. With its withered flowers and suffering wooden saints lurking in the alcoves, it seemed a sinister place to live with children and to have a love affair. The guidebook told me that she had no choice but to rent rooms here, because no one dared offer accommodation to Chopin who had been diagnosed with tuberculosis. I admired her for trying to keep cheerful for her children and writing at her desk wearing Chopin's trousers instead of wasting her life weeping about her circumstances. With this in mind, I briskly walked out of the monastery and made my way through the almond trees towards the silver sea, fierce and roaring beyond the cliffs.

As the waves crashed on the rocks and the wind numbed my fingers, I waited for something to happen. I think I was waiting for a revelation, something big and profound that would shake me to the core. Nothing happened. Nothing happened at all. And then what came to mind was the poster in my bathroom called 'The Skeletal System' which I had misread as 'The Societal System'. The second thing that came to mind was the mute piano in Maria's hallway, a piano that was polished every day but never played. I don't know why it preoccupied me, but it had caught my attention. In fact I had tried not to look at it on my way down the stairs that morning. I thought about all the things I had hoped for and I laughed. The sound of my own cruel laughter made me want to die.

Later that evening, when I asked Maria's belligerent brother for an extra blanket to get me through another night in freezing Majorca, he pretended not to understand me. I could smell wood smoke all over the valley and it was obvious to me that every house had a fire going. Sure enough the one restaurant open out of season had a log fire burning at the back of the room and I made my way towards it. When the waitress came to tell me that noooo waaaay could I sit alone at a table laid for three, I took a tip from Maria's brother and pretended not to understand her. This prompted the German couple sitting nearby wearing identical hats, coats and walking boots to translate what she was saying into German, then Portuguese, and finally a language that sounded like Russian. I concentrated on the menu with incredible focus, nodding annoyingly at the furious waitress and earnest linguists, until I noticed the Chinese shopkeeper was sitting in the bar. He waved and walked over to my table for three.

So, he asked me, did I still think the Majorcans were lucky to meet a lewd and discourteous woman like Jorge Sand?

I told him, yes, they were very lucky to meet her and I was lucky to meet him too because I was just

23

about to be dragged away from my table by the fire. He sat down and explained that even though she came from the sophisticated cuisine of France where everyone cooked with butter, it is not right to mock peasants for cooking in cheap oil, as she did. His accent became more Chinese than Spanish when he said that. It was as if his voice had suddenly dropped from one altitude to another, like turbulence on an aeroplane. I invited him to share a bottle of wine at my table for three.

At first we talked about soup. He told me he had more or less forgotten how to make Chinese soup. Many years ago he had left Shanghai aged nineteen on a ship heading for Paris where he worked in a fish shop. His bedsit in the 13th arrondissement always smelt of the crab and shrimp he cooked most days. This perplexed his landlord who said the room usually smelt of urine – as if that was what was required in Paris. Europe was mysterious and crazed. He had to learn a new language and earn his rent, but it was the start of another way of living and he was excited every day. Now he sold calzone and bratwurst to tourists and he was richer, but he wondered what else there was to look forward to? I think he was asking me a question but I did not want to answer it. He took a small sip of wine and placed his glass neatly, almost surgically on the table. And then he lifted up his hand, and with his two fingers outstretched, briskly tapped my arm.

'You're a writer, aren't you?'

It was not exactly a straightforward question because a few years back I'd glimpsed him reading one of my books behind the sweating cheeses laid out for tourists on the counter of his shop. He knew I was a writer, so I wondered what it was he actually wanted to know. I sensed he was asking me something else. I think I had been asking myself something else too because I was still no closer to figuring out why I had been crying on escalators. So when he said, 'You're a writer aren't you,' what came to mind again was the poster of the Skeletal System in my bathroom. I wasn't sure my skeletal system had found a way of walking freely in the Societal System – for a start it had proved quite tricky to be alone at night in an empty restaurant and be allowed to sit at a table. If I had been George Sand, I would have thrown my cigar butt on the floor, sat myself down at a table laid for six and loudly ordered a suckling pig and a flagon of finest red wine. But that was not the sort of drama I wanted. The night before, when I had walked in to the forest at midnight, that was what I really wanted to do. I was lost because I had missed the turning to the hotel, but I think I wanted to get lost to see what happened next.

I still hadn't answered the Chinese shopkeeper's question, 'You're a writer aren't you?' That spring, when life was very hard and I simply could not see where there was to get to, it was impossible to say

yes, or hmmm, or even to nod. I suppose I was embarrassed at what I was thinking. Anyway, it would
have been such a long answer; something like this:
'When a female writer walks a female character in
to the centre of her literary enquiry (or a forest) and
this character starts to project shadow and light all
over the place, she will have to find a language that is
in part to do with learning how to become a subject
rather than a delusion, and in part to do with unknot-
ting the ways in which she has been put together by
the societal system in the first place. She will have to
be canny how she sets about doing this because she
will have many delusions of her own. In fact it would
be best if she was uncanny when she sets about doing
this. It's exhausting to learn how to become a subject,
it's hard enough learning how to become a writer.'

I didn't know how to join these thoughts up
and there was still a part of me that did not want
to spend another second of my life thinking (again)
about all of this stuff. So I left these thoughts hang-
ing like a wave waiting to crash and I still had not
answered the Chinese shopkeeper's question.

He tapped my arm again. And then he poured
more wine in to my glass. His eyes were clear and
kind. He was inviting me to speak and I could sense
that he was angling for the long story, rather than
a yes or no or even a hmm or a shrug. I thought I
had nothing to lose by telling him about crying on
escalators.

He said, look you know I can speak Spanish and I can speak French too. But my English is not so good. Can you speak Chinese?

No.

Can you speak French or Spanish?

No.

So why do you English people speak no languages?

That's true, I said, but do you know I am not completely English either? He was surprised to hear that and the waitress with her fierce and roaring eyes who was eavesdropping nearby looked surprised too. Of course his next question was to ask me where I was born? I started to speak to the Chinese shopkeeper in English about where I was born, but I'm not sure I went on to say everything you're going to read now.

Two

– Historical Impulse –

I have gradually come to understand what every great
philosophy until now has been; the confession of its author
and a kind of involuntary unconscious memoir.
– Friedrich Nietzsche, *Beyond Good and Evil* (1886)

1 JOHANNESBURG, 1964

I t's snowing in apartheid South Africa. It's snowing on a zebra and it's snowing on a snake. It's
snowing on my father's spectacles and for a moment
I can't see his eyes. I am five years old and have only
seen snow in picture books. My father takes my
hand and we walk down the steps of the red verandah and into the garden to take a closer look at our
peach tree. It is covered in ice crystals. We are going to build a snowman even though we don't own
gloves or warm scarves, but never mind, says Dad,
let's get going, it doesn't snow every day in Africa.

First we make the body, scooping handfuls of
miraculous Johannesburg snow and patting it into a
fat dome. Last of all we make the snowman's head,
tracing a wide smile with a stick that had fallen from
the peach tree. What shall we do for eyes? I run into
the house and come back with two ginger biscuits.

We poke out the holes and press the round gingers into the snow head. When it gets dark we make our way back inside our rented bungalow in the suburb of Norwood, up the wax-polished steps that leads to the red doep that leads to a door that opens into the kitchen where a cotton sack of oranges leans against the peeling paint of the pantry wall.

Outside, the snowman stood under the African stars. Tomorrow we would make him even taller and fatter and find him a scarf.

That night while I lay in bed, the special branch of the security police knock on the door of our bungalow. They want my father and tell him to pack a suitcase. Two of the policemen are smoking cigarettes in the garden, watched by the snowman whose eyes are round and hollow. The suitcase my father is packing is very small. Does that mean he will be back soon? The men have their big hands on his shoulders. Dad is trying to smile at me. A smile like the snowman's that turns up at the corners. And now he is being marched off at a pace by men who I know from conversations overheard between Mom and Dad torture other men and sometimes have swastikas tattooed on their wrists. A car is parked outside the house. The men are saying COM COM COM. The white car pulls away with my father in-side it. I wave but he doesn't wave back.

When I walk into the garden in my pajamas I ask the snowman a question. I speak to him like people speak to God, I talk to him in my head and he answers me.

'What is going to happen?'

The snowman tells me: 'Your father will be thrown into a dungeon and tortured and he will scream all night long and you will never see him again.'

I can feel someone stroking my hair. Now the large brown hands of Maria cover my face, her palms pressing in to my cheeks. Maria is a tall Zulu woman who has a secret stash of chewy oblong sweets called Pinkies wrapped in waxy paper hidden in her pocket. Maria is crying too and she is saying, 'If you don't believe in apartheid you can go to prison. You have to be brave today and tomorrow and so do lots of children have to be brave because their fathers and mothers have been taken away too.'

Maria lives with us and she is my nanny. She has a daughter my age called Thandiwe but Maria says Thandiwe's other name is Doreen so the whites can say her name. Maria's real name is Zama. I can say Zama but she says to call her Maria, which my mother says is a Spanish and Italian name.

'What is Thandiwe doing now, Maria?'

Every time I ask Maria about her own daughter she makes a clicking noise with her tongue. I think the click means STOP, stop asking me about Thandiwe. When we get back to the kitchen, she tells me to rub Vaseline into her feet. Maria always keeps a pot of Vaseline in her pocket as well as the Pinkies. She takes it out now and I sit on the floor so she can put her right foot on my lap. The skin on the back of her heels is dry and cracked which is why I am instructed to 'polish' her feet with the oily jelly until my fingers become hot. At the same time I watch my mother make phone calls to lawyers and friends while my one-year-old brother, Sam, sleeps on her shoulder. When Mom makes a sign with her eyes to Maria, I know she doesn't want me to hear what she is saying.

'What is Thandiwe doing now, Maria?'

A week ago Thandiwe had come to the house and Maria put us both in the bath and scrubbed us with a brand new bar of Lux. We stared at each other and took turns to hold the soap. Maria even gave us both a Pinkie so it must have been a special day and then she put some Vaseline on both our lips because we were all 'cracked up' from the sun. When Thandiwe had to leave the house she cried like a hose pipe that had been slashed. Tears spurted from her eyes onto the towel wrapped around her belly. She cried while her mother held her in her lap and dressed her in the brand new school shoes she had bought from her wages. Her little girl arms that smelt of Lux were wrapped around her mother's neck. Thandiwe was not supposed to be in our house because she was black. I had to promise not to tell anyone, no one at all. Sometimes I called Thandiwe Doreen, sometimes I didn't. Doreen was still crying when Maria left the bungalow to walk her to the 'Blacks Only' bus stop where she would return to where she lived in the 'township'. Maria told her she had to be brave and that her Grandma was waiting to see her new shoes. Watching Thandiwe try to be brave was the worst thing that had happened in my life so far apart from Dad being taken away. I don't know what happened after I had rubbed Vaseline into Maria's feet, but later I was in bed and my mother was lying next to me. When our heads touched it was pain and it was also love.

In the morning the snowman had melted. It had disappeared just like Dad.

What is a snowman? He is a round paternal presence built by children to watch over the house. He is weighty, full of substance, but he is also insubstantial, flimsy, spectral. I knew from the moment we gave him ginger biscuits for eyes that he had become a snow ghost.

2

Two years later I was seven years old and Dad was still gone but my mother said he would come back. I stared into my Barbie doll's painted-on eyes and thought about this. My father was gone. He was gone because he was a member of the African

National Congress and the government had banned the ANC because it was fighting for equal human rights. Everyone had to be brave.

I searched Barbie's blue eyes for any signs of her not being brave. To my relief I found none at all because her eyes had been painted on. She was as calm and pretty as it was possible to be and I wanted to be like that too. I was glad my doll came with four wigs and a hair dryer. Barbie was clearly untouched by anything horrible that happened in the world. I wished I had blue eyes that were painted on with long black eyelashes. I wanted eyes that held no secrets (where's your father then?) because there were no secrets to hold (he's in a dungeon being tortured). Barbie was plastic and I wanted to be plastic too.

At school when I tried to speak, it was a big effort to make my words come out loud. The volume of my voice had somehow been turned down and I didn't know how to turn it up. All day I was asked to repeat what I'd just said and I had a go, but repeating things did not make them louder.

'Are yoo dumb?'

I told the children that my father was away in England.

'Where?'

'Ingerland.'

I wasn't sure where England was or where exactly my father was but my Afrikaans teacher stared at me as if she knew everything. I was thinking about the phrase 'out of the blue'. It was so thrilling to think about the blue that things came out of. There was a blue, it was big and mysterious, it was like mist or gas and it was like a planet but it was also a human head which is shaped like a planet. Out of the blue my teacher asked me how I spelt my surname?

L–E–V–Y.

It was obvious to me she knew my father was a political prisoner, but then she said in an excited voice, 'Ja, you are Jewish,' as if she had just discovered something incredible, like a Roman coin stuck in the paw of a kitten or a dragonfly concealed in a loaf of bread. And then she blinked her liver-coloured eyelashes and said, 'I've had enough of your nonsense.'

Her comment did not come out of the blue. Not at all. The clue was that for weeks now, she had written angry things in my exercise book.

ALWAYS WRITE ON THE TOP LINE. START HERE.

I had ignored her red biro correction because writing on the top line was impossible. I did not know why but I always started on the third line so there was a gap between the top of the page and the line I started on. She said I was wasting paper and she had filled up the empty spaces between the first and third line on every page with her own writing.

START HERE.

START HERE.

START HERE.

When she shook her finger at my face it went right through my eye like a ghost slipping through a brick wall.

'Read out loud to me what I've written in your book.'

'Start here.'

'I can't hear you!'

'START HERE.'

'Yes. Why are you the only child in my class who thinks she can start any where she likes? Take your book and go to the headmaster's office. He is expecting you.' That came right out of the blue. I didn't really want Mister Sinclair to expect me.

As I carried the offending exercise book under my arm, I peered through the window into the other classroom. In class 1J there was boy called Piet who had a purple mark on his forehead like a bullet wound. All the children knew that a teacher had shaved his hair and dabbed iodine onto his forehead with a ball of cotton wool because he swore in class. Now his forehead was stained purple so everyone could see he had done something wrong. I wondered whether the mark would ever go away. When I learned about Jesus Christ and the way nails were hammered through the palms of his poor carpenter's hands I thought of Piet. Would he walk around for the rest of his life with a hole in his head just like Jesus who came back to life with holes in his hands?

I could see Piet through the window, his milky white forehead stained with the purple mark while his finger traced words on the page. Would Lux take off the purple stain or had it gone in too deep?

Piet was Afrikaans and I knew that the COM COM COM men who had taken my father away were Afrikaners too. I had a vague idea that I was supposed to think that Afrikaners were bad people but I felt truly sorry for Piet. And then I remembered I had done something wrong too and I had to walk over the concrete bridge to the headmaster's office.

The bridge looked over the playground. All the white children were in their classrooms but three black children, two boys and a girl, had climbed over the gate and were turning over the dustbins. The African children were barefoot and the girl was wearing a yellow dress with only one sleeve. Her hair was cut close to her head like Thandiwe's hair. Sometimes Thandiwe and I washed each other's hair in the bath with the slab of Lux. When we got soap in our eyes we had to splash our faces with water and try and find a towel with our eyes shut. We bumped in to each other because the stinging soap had blinded us but we were not as blind as we pretended to be. We liked to bump in to each other. From my view on the bridge I could see that the girl had found some bread and one of the boys had found a green sock. He put it in his pocket. And then he looked up and saw me watching him. When he looked up I ducked, then straightened my knees and peered over the bridge again. The children had run away and Mr Sinclair was expecting me.

'Show me your book.'

The headmaster sat at his desk drinking a cup of coffee.

My hands moved the exercise book towards him, sliding it across the shiny table. He opened the book and stared at the first page. Then he turned the page over and the page after that too. Mr Sinclair was frowning. I could see his finger pointing to the top line. A tuft of black hair sprouted from his knuckle as he tapped the page with START HERE written all over it.

'Here. Why don't you start here? Here. Here. Here. You start here. Do you understand?'

When I nodded my two blonde pony tails bounced from side to side.

He stood up and began to roll up the cuffs of his shirt sleeves. A framed photograph of two children stood on his desk. A boy and a girl. The boy's hair had been shaved like Piet's and he was wearing a scout's uniform. The girl wore a blue gingham dress and had a matching blue band in her lovely ginger hair. Suddenly I felt Mr Sinclair's hands on my legs. It made me jump it was so unexpected. The headmaster was slapping the backs of my legs with his hands.

There was something I was beginning to understand at seven years old. It was to do with not feeling safe with people who were supposed to be safe. The clue was that even though Mr Sinclair was white and a grown-up and had his name written in gold letters on the door of his office, I was definitely less safe with him than I was with the black children I had been spying on in the playground. The second clue was that the white children were secretly scared of the black children. They were scared because they threw stones and did other mean things to the black children. White people were afraid of black people because they had done bad things to them. If you do bad things to people, you do not feel safe. And if you do not feel safe, you do not feel normal. The white people were not normal in South Africa. I had heard all about the Sharpeville Massacre that happened a year after I was born and how the white police shot down the black children and women and men and how it rained afterwards and the rain washed the blood away. By the time Mr Sinclair said, 'Go back to your class room,' he was panting and sweating and I could tell he did not feel normal.

Clutching the book that had got me into so much trouble I decided not to return to my class room. I walked straight out of the school gates and made my way to the park where I swung on a rubber tyre tied with rope to a tree. A sign painted in red enamel nailed onto the fence spelt: 'This play park

for European children only. By order town clerk.'
The sun was scorching my bare knees so I moved to
the seesaw which was in the shade and stayed there
for two hours.

When I got home I took an orange from the sack
in the pantry and rolled it under the sole of my bare
foot until it was soft. Then I made a hole in it with
my thumb and sucked out the juice. I was still thirsty
so I drank water from the hose pipe in the yard. It
was the hottest time of the day and our tomcat had
collapsed under the peach tree that had once, mi-
raculously, been covered in snow. At six o'clock my
mother got back from work and said she needed to
talk to me. It was obvious the school had rung her to
say I hadn't turned up for the afternoon because she
told me I was going to stay for a few months with my
Godmother who lived in Durban. After she hugged
me for a long time, I walked back in to the garden
to tell Maria .

Maria always sat on the steps of the verandah
at night and drank condensed milk from a little tin
she had pierced with the can opener. She said she
was looking out for the parktown prawns. Sam and I
had planted ten watermelon seeds in the garden but
Maria had told us the parktown prawns might get
to eat the young melons before we did. She said the
parktown prawn was actually a king cricket and it
attacked the rotting peaches that has fallen from our
tree. If we touched one it would leap at us and spray

a jet black liquid in to our eyes. When I sat next to her on the steps, she put some Vaseline on my lips and asked if everything was alright at school? I shook my head and she sat me on her lap but I knew she was tired and wanted to drink her sweet milk and be alone. She said the stars were so bright she would be able to see if the parktown prawns flew in and if they did she would see them off. Then she gave me a handful of Pinkies from her pocket and said I must tell her about Godmother Dory's new budgie when I came home. Apparently the budgie was called Billy Boy. I liked the way Maria said, 'Godmother Dory'. Was that called a phrase? I resolved that when I got to Durban, I wouldn't say Dory, I would say, Godmother Dory. It didn't sound quite right when I said it to myself. In fact every time I said Godmother Dory out loud, that combination of words felt uncomfortable – as if I was walking around with three little stones in my plimsolls. For some reason I did not want to take out the stones.

At the end of the week, a smart air hostess with a big diamond on her finger led me up the stairs to the aeroplane and told me to suck my thumb as soon as the plane took off for Durban.

'Diamonds are a girl's best friend,' the hostess winked. 'One day when you get married your fiancé will give you a rock too.' When her eye flickered, the diamond on her finger flickered too. 'If the plane crashes I'll blow my whistle okay?' Sitting alone sucking my thumb, I waited for her to blow the whistle but she was too busy walking up and down the aisle showing passengers her engagement ring.

Later she said, 'Look, that's Maputaland, can you see the lakes and marshes? That's Rocktail Bay where my lover boy proposed to me. It's got a coral reef. Nearly in Durban. You must ask your daddy to drive you to the game reserve and show you the lions and elephants okay?'

I nodded.

'Hey, don't you speak?'

I shook my head.

'Left your tongue in Jo'burg?'

I nodded.

'Is that the pilot calling me? It is isn't it? Hope the wing hasn't fallen off!'

She winked and made her way towards the cockpit where the pilot was smoking a cigar. It was his birthday and the crew were singing a rugby song:

She had no clothes on at all
at all at all at all
she had no clothes on at all

3

Godmother Dory presided like a gaoler over Billy Boy's existence.

He couldn't get back to his bird world because he was locked up in his cage. When he played on his ladder and swing he lifted his wings while he whizzed in the air but it wasn't the same as flying.

'Shut that window otherwise Billy Boy will fly away. You can hold him in your hands. Do you want to?'

I nodded.

'He makes more noise than you do.'

When I cupped Billy Boy in my hands and buried my nose in his soft feathers, the pilot's rugby song came in to my head.

He had no feathers on at all
at all at all at all
he had no feathers on at all

Poor Billy Boy. He was so sad under his feathers. His small organs and little bones. Godmother Dory told me to count his toes every month. Apparently if a budgie had some of its toes missing this was because of mites. And I had to listen to him breathe. If there was a 'click' when he took a breath that meant he had air sac mites. Godmother Dory knew everything there was to know about budgies. She told me that it was very important not to take pity on a sick budgie for sale in a pet shop.

'Pity will not bring a sick budgie back to life. It will die of respiratory problems whatever you do.'

I tried to slap down the pity I felt for Billy Boy

in case it killed him but it kept coming back. I stared at the sawdust at the bottom of his cage and told myself he was happy and well but I didn't believe myself. As far as I was concerned all the crops had failed to grow in Billy Boy's life and any hope he possessed had been eaten by ants and his parents had been crushed by a train.

I had forgotten how huge my Godmother was. When she hugged me, I disappeared in to the folds of her stomach. Everything went dark and muffled and I could hear the water dripping inside her pipes. A rumbling noise that was like the sea which was five miles away from the house. The Indian ocean. A sea full of sharks. The life guards on the Golden Mile, which was what the beach was called, had to check the shark nets every morning and make announcements on tannoys when it was not safe to swim. I'd already had to run out of the water and wait on the sand until the shark had been caught. While they were catching the shark I read the signs on the beach:

CITY OF DURBAN
THIS BATHING AREA IS RESERVED FOR THE
SOLE USE
OF MEMBERS OF THE WHITE RACE

The only black people allowed onto the beach were the ice cream sellers who walked barefoot across the hot sand, ringing a bell, shouting, 'Eski-mo pie, choc-ice, eskimo pie.' Sometimes the white boys who went surfing had a leg chewed off if they went too far out on their boards and my Godmoth-er would show me their picture in the newspaper the next day. She said she was more scared of tape-worms than sharks. When the ginger cat was sick on the carpet she flung up her arms and screamed because she said there might be a tapeworm in the vomit. The maid called Caroline cleaned it up while Madam shut her eyes and squealed, her soft white hand clamped over her lips. It seemed then that a tapeworm could swallow a shark; fear did not have a logical size and what's more, fear was a *hermaphro-dite*. My Godmother told me that tapeworms have both male and female organs in their long long bod-ies: 'They have ovaries and testes all mixed in to-gether,' they are 'hermaphrodites', and if that wasn't terrifying enough, 'Any human being who likes to eat raw meat should know that a tapeworm would like to eat them.'

Outside the house in Durban, wired onto the gate, was a big sign:

ARMED RESPONSE

When I asked what it meant my Godmother who knew everything was happy to explain: 'If The Blacks break into the house and rob us, my hus-

45

band, the venerable Edward Charles William, will shoot them, but don't tell your mother. So while you stay with us you needn't worry about a thing!' So far I'd been introduced to sharks, tapeworms and guns. And hermaphrodites. And orchids. 'Come and look at the flowers in my garden. My orchids have small blooms but smell stronger than the bigger ones.'

It was in Godmother Dory's garden in sub-tropical Durban that a miracle lay in wait for me, a hallucination, a mirage, a sort of cartoon. Leaning against the palm tree under Natal's blue sky, smacking flies off her long tanned legs, was a living Barbie doll. Something was shining in the sunshine. It was a gold letter in the shape of an M and the M was attached to a gold chain she wore around her neck. I was dazzled. Somehow, Godmother Dory had managed to produce a slim, blonde daughter who looked like plastic.

'Hello. I'm Melissa. I've just got back from a shorthand course in Pretoria. Aren't you going to say hello to me? You're not in church, you can speak loud you know.'

Just as tiny Barbie was losing her aura and becoming a mere toy with nylon hair, a living Barbie wearing a pastel blue mini-skirt had appeared on the scene.

'C'mon baby. Sit in my bedroom and talk to me.'

Melissa was seventeen, wore her hair in a beehive

and painted her eyelashes with a little brush which she dipped in a pot of black mascara.

'Hey don't you speak? Aaaah. You don't have to. But listen I'm doing my secretarial exams. I got to do shorthand, so if you talk fast I can practise writing what you say. It's a code called Pitman's.' Melissa took out a pen and wrote some squiggles on the back of my hand. 'It says, Welcome to Durbs my little chum.'

It was an honour to be allowed to sit on Melissa's bed and witness the way she teased her hair with a plastic comb until it stood on end all over her head. A special crystal ashtray lay under the bed. I could just see it under the white pom-poms that shivered on the edge of the pink satin eiderdown. Melissa was a secret smoker and kept the ashtray under her bed to hide the butts from her mother. The best moment was when I got to spray the slim can of gold lacquer all over her beehive while she peeped through her half-closed eyes, lashes stiff with mascara. The sweet chemical vapour from the lacquer was like a painkiller. I watched Melissa make herself up in awed, humble silence. The idea that plastic people were the most interesting people was born first of all in Barbie's painted-on blue eyes, then in Maria's painted on brown eyes every time I asked about Thandiwe, and finally in Melissa's teenage laboratory. Melissa was quite literally making herself up. The fact that lipstick and mascara and eye shadow were called 'Make Up' thrilled me. Everywhere in the world there were made up people and most of them were women.

'Hey dumb girl, let me do your hair for you. Sit on my lap and I'll make you a lekker style.'

With Melissa's help my sad, sensible pony tail soon changed into an exotic coil of golden plaits pinned on top of my head. Melissa said I looked like a movie star and all I needed were some diamonds and rubies to put in my ears and drape round my neck and weave round my wrists. Emeralds would suit me best because of my green eyes. When I had daughters of my own, I would give them my emeralds because they would have 'served their purpose'. What was their purpose?

She said I was a 'beauty' and one day, if I remembered to scrub my fingernails clean, a dashing man would take my hand and he would kiss it with his lips for a long time. Then he would kneel at my feet while I looked down at his hair parting and he would beg me to be his wife. I hoped that I would be like Melissa when I grew up. I too would smoke cigarettes and be able to make squiggles on paper in Pitman's code and drive barefoot in fast cars with my stilettos chucked on the back seat for later.

'Never wear shoes when you drive my little chum, that's the best way.'

But first of all I had to tiptoe past her one-eyed father and make myself invisible to him. Edward

Charles William had one glass eye and one real eye. Melissa told me that when he was a boy someone poked out his left eye in a rugby game and now his eyes did not match. The glass eye had purple flames in it. It was practically a fire burning in his socket. I made up a rule: only look at his glass eye. Never ever catch sight of his real eye. A glass eye was an unseeing eye and I did not want him to see that I was frightened of him. Edward Charles William was like a king. When he sat at the head of the table with his wife and only daughter, I could see us all reflected in his glass eye, I could even see the grey dog called Rory wagging his tail and panting in Edward Charles William's eye.

'ROOOREEEEE! Sit! Sit!'

'Pa-aa. Uch Pa you're frightening the wits out of my new little chum! Just ignore him dumb girl, he's a pussy cat.' Melissa shook her pink frosted finger nail at her father, winking at him while she filled his glass with scotch and sent me into the kitchen to get his ice.

While I was in the kitchen I stared out of the window while the ice cubes melted in my hands. The ice reminded me of building the snowman with my father. I was going to be eight years old soon and he still hadn't come home. When I returned to the table and Edward Charles William looked furious at the sight of the tiny slivers of ice that were dripping in my hot hand. Melissa covered up for me.

'Pa, ugh, Pa, why is it so hard to find ice that doesn't melt in three seconds? What's the science, Pa?'

If I had anything to ask my own father I would have to ask him in my head. When Melissa said, 'Will you take me fishing?' and her father said 'Yes,' I asked my father if he would take me fishing too? His ghostly answer was always, 'Fishing is treacherous. You might get the hook stuck in your finger!' Or I would say, 'Dad, today I climbed to the very top of the tree,' and he would say, 'Climbing trees is treacherous. Don't climb all the way up. Climb halfway and never look down!'

I guessed that Edward Charles William did not want me to be living with them in Durban but Godmother Dory told me that it was necessary for me to have 'a stable home' and that it was 'the least she could do' because she and my 'poor poor' mother had gone to boarding school together and they had taken it in turns to keep watch when they read books at midnight under the sheets with a torch.

I began to listen to how Edward Charles William spoke English, which was the language we all spoke. When he wanted his socks, he yelled at a servant to get them for him. When he wanted a towel for his evening shower he yelled again. He didn't say the words socks or towel he just yelled the name of the servant. The name of his servant meant get me my socks, get me a towel.

When his shoes needed polishing, the man who did the garden polished them for him. Edward Charles William called him 'boy' even though he had four children and nine grandchildren and had silver hair. His name was Joseph and he called Edward Charles William, 'Master'. The language Edward Charles William spoke to Joseph was the English language but his tone was like a whole separate language. For a start (and I never knew where to start) I could hear that Edward Charles William's tone was enjoying something too much. I could hear that Edward Charles William needed to be less happy. This thought made me laugh, and every time I laughed I felt a bit happier, which was confusing my new idea about happiness not always being a good thing but there was nothing I could do about it.

One Sunday, Joseph gave me half his pie with gravy and we sat on the grass in the shade because 'Madam and Master' always went for a drive on Sundays. That was the first time I noticed he had two fingers missing from his left hand. When I asked him what happened to his fingers, he said he caught them in a door. He taught me to count to two in Zulu. One was Ukunye, two was Isibili. Or something sing-song like that. The idea that there was a door somewhere in South Africa with Joseph's two fingers stuck in it began to torment me. Later, when I told him that my father was a political prisoner, he told me that an Alsatian dog had bitten off his two fingers when the police raided his brother's house in Jo'burg. They were looking for Nelson Mandela. When I told him my mother and father knew Winnie and Nelson Mandela (who was in prison FOR LIFE on Robben Island) he instructed me not to ever tell this to Madam and Master – or even Billy Boy. And any way, he said, mopping up his pie and gravy with his thumb and two remaining fingers, what was the point of keeping a bird if it didn't lay eggs? Amaqanda. That was Zulu for eggs. If Madam's blue bird laid a blue egg, that would be a little meal.

Every night a grey blanket was placed over Billy Boy's cage. I knew my father slept with a grey blanket over him too because he had told my mother in a letter.

'Come here my little chum, you're freaking me out the way you're always staring at Ma's budgie.' Melissa clasped her arms around my waist and lifted me off the carpet.

'Now say after me, I CAN SPEAK LOUD.'

'I can speak loud.'

'SAY IT LOUDER.'

'I can speak loud.'

'THAT'S NOT LOUD. I'm not putting you down till you scream.'

I experimented with a tiny scream. It sounded quite real and she put me down.

'Lisss-ten, when you smile I know you don't

mean it. Smile for me with all your teeth. Ah that's lekker. Let's take the spaceship into town.'

The spaceship was Godmother Dory's brand new car. She had grown so large she could no longer fit into the old one. I sometimes saw her in the kitchen at night lifting fistfuls of minced meat and potatoes into her little cupid lips. The spaceship was silver and shiny and had spotless cream leather seats. What if the tyres of the new car exploded and Godmother Dory crashed and no one was able to lift her up to take her to hospital?

'Why is your Ma so fat?'

Melissa lunged towards me and stamped hard on my toe. And then she punched my shoulder.

'Don't be so rude, dumb girl. Ma's a prisoner in her own flesh. She can't get out of there.'

'Why not?'

'She's dead but she came back as a zombie.'

'No!'

'You know Jesus is a zombie too? He died and came back to life.'

Melissa waved the car keys in my face.

'Say sorry and I'll buy you a bunny chow.'

'What's a bunny chow?'

'It's lekkkkker. But you don't tell anyone where I'm taking you. Especially Pa. Okay?'

'Okay.'

'You said that nice and loud. Girls have to speak up cuz no one listens to them anyway.'

If Melissa had a secret life, I expected nothing less of a plastic person. Plastic people had things to hide and what Melissa was hiding was that she knew places to eat downtown where her Indian boyfriend lived. This place turned out to be a cafe in a side street full of garbage and flies. Old meat bones lay heaped in the gutter underneath a pile of potato peel and rotting carrots. When we walked into the cafe an Indian man reading a newspaper at the till looked up and shouted, 'Hey Lissa! Is it bunny time?' He was chewing something that had stained his teeth orange. When the man shouted, 'Hey Lissa!' the Indian families devouring plates of curry with their fingers all looked up and then looked down. I guessed they looked down because we were white and not supposed to be there.

'Thanks Victor. And a bunny for my little chum too. She's from Jo'burg.'

Melissa steered me to one of the tables and said, 'Sit.' I was furious when she told me to sit, as if I was a disobedient dog. She had some of her father's tone in her, that was for sure. Melissa had caught 'Master's' tone, she needed to take an aspirin and sweat it out of her. I started to sneeze. Victor carried over a can of Fanta and opened it for me while I was still sneezing.

'So you're from Jo'burg ?'

'Yes.'

'Is Ajay in today?' Melissa interrupted us in her new tone.

Victor pointed at someone with his finger which was also stained orange. A young Indian man had just walked into the cafe. He wore a shiny grey suit and snakeskin shoes and he smiled when he saw Melissa.

'I'll get your bunnies.' Victor made his way across the sawdust on the floor, kicking an empty cigarette packet under a table.

A bunny chow turned out to be meat curry spooned inside the crust of half a white loaf of bread. I ate it with a soup spoon and watched Melissa flirt with Victor's son. Ajay was shrugging, saying something about 'next Tuesday' while Melissa rolled her painted-on eyes up to the ceiling. Ajay lit her cigarette and then he lit his cigarette and they both made O's of smoke in the air. Their O's were the most beautiful thing in the world. Sometimes they floated towards each other and just as they were about to touch they melted in to the air. The air smelt of rice. And spices. The O's and the rice and the spices and the space between Melissa and Ajay whose shoes were made from snake and Melissa whose eyelashes were sooty with mascara and the way her little finger was touching the cuff of Ajay's shirt seemed to me how life could be when it was going well.

When Victor walked back to our table and sat down he ruined it all because he started to talk about politics. Melissa told him how my father was in gaol because of apartheid. Victor told me that his grandfather had come from India to work in the sugar cane fields in Natal. He said every time I sprinkled a teaspoon of sugar on my grapefruit and made my teeth rrrrrotten as a result, I must remember it was his granddad who planted South Africa's white gold - and I must tell my Dad there was always a bunny chow waiting for him in his 'establishment'. I nodded and pretended to be interested but I was really looking at Melissa who was holding Ajay's hand under the table. If this was love, it was forbidden love. Even I knew that. Everyone in the café knew that. Politics had found its way in to grapefruits and into holding hands. I was fed up with politics and looked forward to the day I could smoke and make O's in the rice-scented air and run my little finger under a handsome man's shirt cuff.

When we got to the car park, Melissa took off her sandals and asked me to hold them for her while she searched for the car keys. She never drove in shoes, this was her 'specialty'; her boyfriends always clasped her shoes tightly to their chests while she pressed her bare feet on the gas and sang 'golden hits' by The Shangri-Las.

'Oh maaaan – I think I've left them in Victor's Bunny House!' While she searched frantically in her bag, I gazed at the car parked next to the spaceship. A girl my age was sitting on the back seat holding something on her lap. Her lips were moving, as if she was speaking to someone but no one was there.

'Look she's talking to herself.'

Melissa walked across the oily concrete in her bare feet and peered into the Bentley.

'You know what?'

'What?'

'She's talking to a rabbit!'

'A bunny chow?'

'No. A REAL rabbit.'

It was true. The girl had a white rabbit on her lap. I could just see its ears poking up, tickling the girl's chin. At the same time a man and a woman walked towards the car, the man flicking his keys against his hip. As soon as he unlocked the door, the girl's lips stopped moving. The woman saw us and laughed but she didn't mean it.

'We just took her rabbit to the vet. He's got a sticky eye.'

Her husband made a high pitched voice, like his wife, and repeated what she had just said.

'HE'S GOT A STICKY EYE! HE'S GOT A STICKY EYE.'

When his wife's cheeks reddened, he said it all over again.

He didn't sound like her at all. I wondered who he thought he was imitating? The high voice inside him did not sound like my mother or Maria or me or Melissa or even the woman it was supposed to be. Here was the clue. He sounded like himself.

'HERE THEY ARE!' Melissa's car keys had

somehow slipped inside the Pitman's code book she always carried around with her.

'HOPE YOUR LITTLE BUNNY'S BETTER,' she yelled at the girl. She put her bare foot down on the gas and eased the spaceship out of the car park.

'What do you think she was saying to her rabbit?'

'Ja. Well. That's her secret.'

'Why's it a secret?'

Melissa shrugged, her painted-on eyes fixed on the road as she turned right onto a concrete flyover. It began to thunder.

Naked African children were begging at the traffic lights, hands stretched out, palms turned up.

'What secret was she saying to her rabbit?'

Warm rain started to lash the car windows.

'She said, "Why don't Ma and Pa love each other?"'

4

I knew that smiling was like the magic charms that some girls wore on bracelets. Little silver pixies and hearts jiggling on their suntanned wrists to bring them luck and ward off the evil eye. Smiling was a way of keeping people out of your head even though you'd opened your head when you parted your lips.

This is how I smiled when Godmother Dory told me she was going to send me to the local convent school. While she was saying this she held a little pair of scissors in her hand to trim Billy Boy's wings.

'The feathers should be shiny and full.' Her plump finger prodded Billy Boy's chest. 'This is the keel bone. It's sticking out a little bit more than it should. I think Billy Boy is underweight. I'm going to give him more seed than usual tonight.'

'What's a convent school?'

'It's a school where the teachers are nuns.'

'What's a nun?'

'A nun is a woman who has married Jesus Christ.'

'Oh. The hostess on the plane to Durbs was getting married. She showed me her ring.'

'But she didn't marry Jesus Christ. She probably married a man called Henk van de Plais or something like that. It's quite quite different.'

Her face was pale like a zombie.

'An alert and playful budgie is a sign of a healthy budgie. Billy Boy is not as chirpy as usual.'

When she had finished tidying up Billy Boy's feathers she locked him up again in his cage. I watched how she wiggled the little lever to shut him in so that I could wiggle it to get him out.

'The convent is called Saint Anne's and the nuns are very good teachers. Please take the cat and his tapeworm away from Billy Boy's cage.'

I picked up the cat and warmed my hands in its ginger fur. I knew he didn't have a tapeworm. Maybe Godmother Dory had a tapeworm inside her? The clue was that she was hungry all the time, so something was eating her up. The cat had taken to sleeping in my bedroom. Melissa threatened to cut Ginger's ear off if he didn't return to her pink satin eiderdown, but he had obviously decided to risk it. Ginger Was Mine. When Melissa had been a pupil at the convent she hated it. Now that she was doing a secretarial course and drank Rock Shandy's and met her girl friend from Pietermaritzburg at the Three Monkeys or the Wimpy Burger Bar, she had stopped praying.

'You don't want the Convent girls to think you're a freak do you?'

'No.'

'Then you must speak loud. Hey I'll tell you one thing: you'll be the only girl with a Jewish surname on the register. If you get lost in the cloisters just follow your nose.' Melissa laughed until her painted-on eyes ran all over her face and I joined in because I was her little chum.

Saint Anne's was a provincial school for well-heeled, white-skinned Catholic girls. Between the cloisters stood a small bowed statue of the Madonna and child, the sad mother with her baby in her arms. On the streets of Durban most African mothers carried their babies strapped to their backs but if they were looking after the white babies they pushed them in a pram. Did the Madonna have a servant to hold her baby for her? I wondered if my own mother was missing me? I hoped so. Perhaps I was a saintly orphan who had been sent by God to be cared for by the nuns? I leaned against a stone pillar and gazed at a plaster statue of Jesus Christ with slashed hands. It made me think all over again about Piet in my Johannesburg school. Had his iodine stigmata faded away yet?

The nuns seemed to have devoted their lives to helping me learn how to read and write. Every day they knelt by my side in the class room, gently rolling plasticine A's and B's and C's in their soft white hands. When they asked me to name the letters, I lowered my head like an orphan saint should do, and whispered 'Ay, bee, sea,' while they nodded encouragingly. I thought it might be rude to tell them I had learned to read and write two years ago. In fact I understood all the signs on the golden mile without the help of plasticine.

THIS BATHING AREA IS RESERVED FOR THE
SOLE USE
OF MEMBERS OF THE WHITE RACE

Sister Joan told me her rosary was threaded in sections of ten beads and the ten beads were called decades. A decade was ten years. What if my father was away for a decade? What if I was swimming in the bathing area reserved for members of the white race for decades but never saw my father again? I would be alone with the white race who were not normal. I would be totally alone with them and at their mercy like the surfers were at the mercy of the Great White Sharks who managed to get through the gill nets in the subtropical sea.

The oldest nun passed me an M.

'M for Melissa', I whispered dutifully.

'Yes, How is Melissa?' Sister Joan was now rolling out an N which I knew came after M. I had known this since I was about four.

'She's at secretarial college.'

'And is she doing well at the tech?'

'She's learning Pitman's code.'

I did not tell Sister Joan that Melissa (two S's in Melissa but we were only on N at the moment) had been banned from driving for a month. This was because she hijacked the spaceship and drove Ajay to see his uncle. Last night when Edward Charles William saw the car was missing at 1.15am he made Godmother Dory wake me up. She dragged me in to the living room and Edward Charles William squeezed his face so close to mine that he squashed my nose.

'Do you know where fat face is?'

I shook my head and stared into his glass eye.

'Is she seeing a boy?'

'No.'

'An Indian boy? '

'No.'

'I'VE GOT A BLARRY KAFFIR LOVER FOR A DAUGHTER! YOU'VE COME TO STAY AT THE RIGHT HOUSE, HEY?'

'Get away from her,' Godmother Dory squealed in a begging sort of way, 'Leave the child alone. What am I to say to her poor mother?' Meanwhile Ginger cat lay asleep on the sofa with its soft paws crossed over each other.

When Edward Charles William put his hand over his glass eye I was terrified it was going to fall out. A sentence formed in my mind. It resembled the sign on the beach:

THIS GLASS EYE IS RESERVED FOR THE
SOLE USE
OF MEMBERS OF THE WHITE RACE

Edward Charles William told me he was going to call the police to find Melissa. The police? The same men who had taken my father away? When the spaceship swerved in to the driveway, Melissa beeped the hooter at the police car that had arrived at the same time as she did, rolled down the window and waved like she was on holiday.

'Hey guys! I didn't steal my ma's spaceship honest. I was abducted.' The policemen laughed but

Melissa went crazy after they left. She called her father 'a fucking Nazi' and told me that now she couldn't drive it was hard to find a place she could meet with Ajay. South Africa was shit, Ginger was shit, Rory was shit and I was a dumb freak.

'Do you still want to be a dolly like your horrible little Barbie?'

'Yes.'

'How can you be a dolly *and* a saint? You know there was a saint called Lucy who plucked out her eyes? But she could still see things because you never stop seeing things until you die. I want to die if I can't see Ajay.'

Sister Joan was now smiling at sister Elizabeth who didn't notice because she was busy making a plasticine O. I nodded piously and copied her smile, which was half a smile, as if she had decided a whole one was going too far. She passed me the O. It reminded me of Melissa and Ajay's smoke rings of love but I said quite loudly, 'O is for orange. There is one O in God and one O in mother.'

'Yes. Well done. And are you happy staying with your godmother?'

Happy? I gazed at my ugly black regulation school shoes. Happy? There were two P's in happy. I could already see Sister Elizabeth rolling out the plasticine P. Perhaps it made the nuns happy to play with plasticine? Perhaps they should roll out plasticine all day long while I read a book? Did they know I actually read books, lots of them, all the way through? Did they think I was dumb like Melissa thought I was dumb? Was I happy? Was I supposed to be happy?

After a while Sister Joan took my hand in her own holy hand and asked me if I believed in God.

The picture of God I held in my mind was connected to the snowman I had built with my father. The snowman was God. He was cold and dead but I thought about him all the time. By way of answering, I opened my satchel and showed her a letter my father had sent to Durban. It occurred to me that I should read it out loud to her so we could stop making plasticine letters.

My darling,

I'm glad the nuns are so nice. Be sure to say your thoughts out loud and not just in your head.

Kisses to the sky.

With all my love from your Daddy.

Sister Joan squeezed my hand.

'When your father says say your thoughts out loud, he means for you to speak louder.'

'Speak louder to God?'

I waited for her to say, yes, but she was silent. That was the first time I understood the phrase, 'Read between the lines.'

I had been told to say my thoughts out loud and not just in my head but I decided to write them down. It was five in the morning and I could hear Rory barking at the reed frogs in the pond. I found a biro and had a go at writing down my thoughts. What came out of the biro and onto the page was more or less everything I did not want to know.

Dad disappeared.
Thandiwe cried in the bath.
Piet's got a hole in his head.
Joseph's fingers got bitten off
Mr Sinclair hit my legs.
The watermelons grew and I wasn't there.
Maria and Mom are far away.
Sister Joan might not believe in God.
Billy Boy behind bars.

Billy Boy was my main thought. I put the biro down and then I opened my bedroom door. I would have to be quiet otherwise Edward Charles William might think I was a burglar and do what was written on the sign outside the house:

ARMED RESPONSE

If I was going to do what was 'between the lines'

of what I had written down, which was to free Billy Boy, then so might Edward Charles William do what was 'between the lines' of the words ARMED RESPONSE. Were words just threats or were they serious? Was it true that sticks and stones were more dangerous than words? What was the point of just writing things down, any way? What was the point of writing, BUY MORE PINKIES, but not buying them because writing it down had replaced the desire to actually buy them?

I crept into the dining room. On the polished table were four bowls, four silver spoons, four cups, an empty toast rack and four china plates. Would Goldilocks have broken in to the bears' cottage if she'd seen a sign on the gate that said ARMED RESPONSE?

I ran past the table and pushed open the door that led to the living room where Billy Boy lived in his cage. First of all I opened the window that looked out over the garden. Then I lifted the grey blanket off the cage. Billy Boy opened his little brown eyes. They were the same colour as my father's eyes. I counted his toes. Yes he had all ten of them so he didn't have mites. Then I listened to him breathe to make sure I didn't hear a click. Last of all I peered at his beak, checking to see the holes weren't clogged up. I wiggled the latch and opened the cage door.

Billy Boy lifted up his wings. And then he closed them tight against his little blue body. He lifted one foot in the air, paused, and put it down on his perch.

Birds everywhere were singing. It seemed to me that all over Natal, birds trilled into the first light of day, encouraging the blue bird to break free and join them.

If I had poured all my childhood anxieties in to Billy Boy's tiny carcass, he had a lot to carry. He was very heavy. I had given him a soul, but he didn't seem to care. I had imagined all kinds of things for Billy Boy, breathed in to him all my secret wishes. I had given him another life to live, but he did not want to be free. He was supposed to be a bird, a flying machine, but he seemed to like his cage more than he liked his liberty. Everything I had imagined for Billy Boy was dead. I didn't know what to do. Betrayed and desolate, I began to walk away from the bird who wanted to spend the rest of his life behind bars.

Something happened. A flutter of wings. The silver cup falling from the mantel shelf. A small dot of blue. A circle of blue. The sweet pea smell coming from the garden. Billy Boy flew out of the window just as the ginger cat padded into the living room, its tail held high in the air.

I pretended everything was normal at breakfast when I sat at the table with my new family. I had been pretending that everything was 'normal' for quite a few years now and had become quite good at it. Edward Charles William crunched his toast and English marmalade while Godmother Dory poured tea from a teapot that was smaller than her bosoms. Today was the day Melissa sat her secretarial exams and she had styled her beehive three inches higher than usual for luck. She was reading her Pitman's textbook while she sipped from a glass of cream soda, which she said would give her energy for the exam. Billy Boy was probably sleeping on a leaf high up in a tree in the morning sunshine.

He was free. Billy Boy was free.

It was only when I was buckling my school regulation shoes that I heard Godmother Dory screaming. I spent more time than usual on the third hole of the buckle, testing it a few times before deciding the second hole was probably a better fit and starting all over again. By the time I made my way towards Godmother Dory, her little hands were flung up in the air and she was calling BILLY BOY over and over again. There were things she wanted to know. How come the cage door was wide open? How can a budgie open its own cage? Melissa who was late for her exam ran to get her mother tissues while trying to put on her white cardigan.

'Don't shout at her.'

'But my little budgie's not going to survive. He's probably dead.'

'You gotta understand Ma,' Melissa was looking for her pad with all the shorthand notes written on it.

'What do I have to understand?'

'She thinks the budgie is her Pa.'

'How can Billy Boy be anything but a budgie?'

If that question was something human beings had been grappling with ever since they started painting animals with mineral pigments on the walls of caves, Melissa's mother had not yet caught up. When Melissa saw me listening outside the living room door she lunged at my school tie and pulled me towards her made up face.

'FUCK YOU. Why did you go and let Ma's bird out?'

Before I could answer she ran off and I heard the engine of the spaceship revving up and the tyres squealing on the drive. Edward Charles William had obviously let Melissa fly the spaceship again because of her exam. After a while I walked into the garden. Joseph was coughing inside his shed. He ate his breakfast there every morning, a thick porridge called mealy meal which the maid called Caroline, who had another name, Nkosiphendule, prepared for him in a tin bowl. I still hadn't managed to buckle my shoe. It was slipping off so I bent down to try again. It was so hard to thread the little silver thing through the hole. After a while, Joseph opened the door of his shed and told me to come in. My shoe was still half on and half off so I had to slide rather than walk. The shed smelt of mould and paraffin. Joseph slept on a mattress on the floor. Two green blankets lay neatly folded on a chair. His jacket hung on a hook in the corner.

'Madam told me you've lost her budgie.'

Madam was Godmother Dory. Master was Edward Charles William. Sometimes Joseph called him Baas as well as Master. Master and Baas and Madam were the white race and they ate kippers and marmalade for breakfast like the King and Queen of Ingerland.

'Look.' Joseph pointed to a wooden crate that he had turned upside down to make a table. On the box was his tin bowl. Billy Boy was hopping up and down on the rim of the bowl, pecking at the porridge inside it.

'I found him on the roof and gave him lodgings.' Joseph started to laugh. 'But he hasn't laid a blue egg yet so we won't be sharing a little meal. I'm going to put a lid on the bowl and you are going to take him back to Madam.'

When I brought Billy Boy back into the house, Madam was lying on the sofa reading a book called *Love Is A Word You Whisper*. The maid who pretended she was Caroline so Madam could say her name carried in a tray with a pot of tea and two strawberry jam biscuits arranged on a saucer. Madam's pudgy fingers moved across the tray and grasped one of the biscuits. I heard her bite in to it and then crunch it with her porcelain teeth. At that moment Billy Boy chirped. Madam sat up and wailed. She had jam all over her little lips and I could see the biscuit crumbs on her tongue. After she had put Billy Boy back into the cage and slammed it shut she walked past me towards the telephone without saying a word. I could hear her asking in a loud royal voice to be put through to South African Airlines.

That afternoon, while I sat on a bench under the cloisters watching the nuns hit the hands of the girls who were being punished for various crimes, I knew that something in my life was about to change. Meanwhile, I observed the choreography of sin and punishment that was happening in front of me because whatever was going to change was going to take me somewhere else. The sinful girl was holding her palm facing upwards, towards heaven. Then the nun took a metre ruler and swiped it across her palm, two whacks, no, three whacks. Sister Joan was busy smelting the hand of an extra sinful girl called Laverne when I saw Godmother Dory waddling through the cloisters. Yesterday, Laverne had shown me a red mark on her neck where her boyfriend had left a love bite. Yes, he had actually bitten her out of love. Sister Joan was talking to my Godmother and she was beckoning to me. Now that she knew all about me letting Billy Boy out of his cage, she was going to purify my hand by beating it.

'Come here.'

To my astonishment, instead of punishing me, Sister Joan bent down and buckled my shoe. She had been teaching me French, the most distinguished thing that had happened in my life so far. She had told me all about the visions of Jeanne d'Arc, and she had taught me the word for shoe. So now she asked me how to say shoe in French. When I said, 'Une chaussure', she stood up and placed her cool clean palm on my forehead.

'Your Godmother says you're homesick so she's sending you back to your mother. This will be your last day at school.'

As my tears dripped on to Sister Joan's holy veil, I thought about how she had shaved off her hair which she called her weeds of ignorance. She had 'told me to say my thoughts out loud but I had tried writing them down instead. Sometimes I showed her what I had written and she always made time to read everything. She said I should have told her I could read and write. Why hadn't I told her? I said I didn't know, and she said I shouldn't be scared of something 'transcendental' like reading and writing. She was on to something because there was a part of me that was scared of the power of writing. Transcendental meant 'beyond', and if I could write 'beyond', whatever that meant, I could escape to somewhere better than where I was now. I was bitten with love for Sister Joan. She had told me that faith was not a rock. God was there one day and gone the next. If that was true, I felt truly sorry for her on the days that she lost God. I searched for the French words for goodbye and when I found them, 'Au revoir Sœur Jeanne,' I realised she had the same name as Joan of Arc. For some reason this made me cry even more. My bemused Godmother who hadn't a clue what was going on snapped open her handbag and took out a scrap of paper.

'Melissa said to give you this.'

It was a note scribbled in Pitman's code.

'Goodbye my crackers little chum.'

6

'Two days to go! Dad's coming home!'

I was now nine years old and Sam five. Sam had last seen his father when he was one. At breakfast we ate toast sprinkled with cinnamon and sugar and practised out loud the sort of things we would say to our father when he walked through the front door.

'Hello. Do you want me to show you the way to the bathroom?'

'Hello! I've drawn you a rocket.'

'Hello! My feet are size three now.'

Meanwhile Mom was out at the shops buying clothes for my father to wear when he came home. My chest went tight when she carefully laid the clothes out on the floor and summoned us to come and have a look. There on the kilim rug were a pair of men's trousers, smart new shoes, socks, two shirts and three brightly coloured ties. Sam and I stroked the cotton of the shirts, pressed our thumbs in to the toes of the leather shoes, adjusted the position of the socks. Yes, these were the sort of things fathers wore. We talked at length about what kind of food we should give our father for his first lunch and Mom said we must try not to be too shy and just be ourselves. We nodded gravely and went off to practise being ourselves.

When Sam went to the park he collected a handful of stompies, cigarette butts that had been ground out on the grass. He saved them in his pockets until he got home and then put them in a little glass jar. Sam was convinced that all dads liked stompies. Maria put on her best dress, the dress she wore when she went home to her house where her real children lived. But before she put on her shoes, she sat down and instructed me to rub Vaseline into the dry skin on her heels.

'Do you know what they found in the Zoo Lake?'

'What?'

'A human head. Put some Vaseline on this leg too.'

'A child's head?'

'No. A man's head.'

'Is it Dad?'

'No. Your father is on his way home.'

I knew my father would be arriving with Mom in a car from Pretoria Central Prison. But I was not sure what he looked like now. To be certain of recognizing him, I held in my lap the black and white photograph my mother had propped up by the telephone in the dark hallway. The photograph that for nearly five years had represented the father who sent his love to me in letters and messages. Kisses and hugs, XXXXX OOOOO written in biro on prison note paper. Sam and I climbed up the two stone gate posts outside their house and I held the photo in my lap, glancing at it every now and again just to make sure. The gateposts were six foot high and looked straight out over the road. Every time a car went past the house we waved. Our hands had been scrubbed clean with a brand new bar of Lux.

For some reason, I thought my father was going to return home in a white car. The same car he was taken away in. So every white car made my heart thump under the white daisies stitched on my dress. The panic of my father not turning up made everything very slow. Clouds moved across the sky slowly. People walked on the pavements slowly. Dogs barked slowly.

A small red car turned left at the golf course and swerved into their road. I stiffened my toes inside my patent shiny shoes and waited. The door opened and a man jumped out and ran towards us. He did not even wait for the car to stop. We knew who it was and I did not bother to look at the photo lying in my lap. It took us a while to get down from the very high gate posts. Dad was waiting for us but we couldn't get down. Now we were all legs and arms and trying to slide down and the man who was our father grabbed our legs and then lifted us in to his arms. He was wearing the shirt we had admired when Mom laid them out in the living room.

Dad hugged us and we didn't know what to say. And then he hugged us again and put us down on the pavement where moss grew in the cracks. We walked through the gate and into the kitchen. When Maria saw him she embraced him and I heard him say the word 'Thandiwe'. Mom poured three glasses of wine, one for Dad, one for Maria and one for her. They raised their glasses and we all looked at Dad. He took a tiny sip, paused and put the glass down again.

'I haven't seen a glass for five years.'

My father was thin and his face was pale. He sat down at the table and sipped his wine again. And then he picked up a plate and ran his finger over it. 'I have forgotten the feel of porcelain. I'll have to learn how to handle a cup again and to manipulate a fork.'

Dad put down the white china plate he has been examining for the last five minutes and stood up.

'Where is the garden?' He cocked his head to one side and smiled at me. 'I want to see the snowman.'

There was no snowman in the garden. Sam wrapped the ends of the new white linen tablecloth around his small wrist and looked down at the floor. Mom tried to remove a fly from the window with the back of an envelope.

'Take your father into the garden.' Maria waved her hands at me.

My father is standing in the garden. His face is pale grey like dirty snow. Only his eyes move. His arms hang stiffly by his sides. Dad is back, so very still and silent, standing in the garden. He looks like he has been hurt in some way. Very deep inside him.

'Daddy, the cat died while you were away.'

He squeezes my hand with his cold fingers.

'It's lovely to be called Daddy again.'

Two months later we left South Africa for the United Kingdom. When the ship pulled away from Port Elizabeth docks in the Eastern Cape province, the passengers were given rolls of toilet paper to unravel from the height of the deck. The other end was held by friends and family standing on dry land waving goodbye. As the ship edged out to sea, Melissa who had come to see me off held the other end of my toilet roll. The ship's hooter wailed into the blue sky. I could see her jumping and shouting but I couldn't hear her. Her words got scrambled in the wind, drowned by the roaring of the tug boats as they pushed the ship out towards England. Melissa was the first person in my life who had encouraged me to speak up. With her blue painted-on eyes and blonde beehive that was nearly as tall as I was, she was spirited and brave and she was making the best of her lot. I couldn't hear her but I knew her words were to do with saying things out loud, owning up to the things I wished for, being in the world and not defeated by it.

I would like to forget the image of the ship's crane at Southampton docks when it lifted into the sky, the three wooden trunks which held all that my family owned. There is only one memory I want to preserve. It is Maria, who is also Zama, sipping condensed milk on the steps of the doep at night. The African nights were warm. The stars were bright. I loved Maria but I'm not sure she loved me back. Politics and poverty had separated her from her own children and she was exhausted by the white children in her care, by everyone and everything in her care. At the end of the day, away from the people who stole her life's energy and made her tired, she had found a place to rest, momentarily, from myths about her character and her purpose in life.

I don't want to know about my other memories of South Africa. When I arrived in the UK, what I wanted were new memories.

Three

– Sheer Egoism –

In the UK greasy spoons are also referred to as 'working
men's cafés', which in the South is often colloquially referred
to as a 'caff' . . . The typical working men's café serves
mainly fried or grilled food, such as fried eggs, bacon,
black pudding, bubble and squeak, sausages, mushrooms
and chips. These are often accompanied by baked beans.

Wikipedia

ENGLAND 1974

When I was fifteen I wore a black straw hat
with square holes punched in the brim and
wrote on paper napkins in the greasy spoon by the
bus station. I had a vague idea this was how writers
were supposed to behave because I had read books
about poets and philosophers drinking espresso in
French cafés while they wrote about how unhappy
they were. There were not many cafés like that in the
UK at the time and certainly not in West Finchley.
In 1974 the miners were on strike, the conservative
government had made a five-day working week a
three-day week to save electricity, China had given
two black and white pandas (Ching-Ching and Chia-
Chia) to the British people – and I was planning

my Saturday morning getaway to the greasy spoon as meticulously as a bank heist. These plans were nearly ruined in a big way by a swarm of suicidal bees. A pot of honey – no lid on it of course, nothing had a lid on it in our house – had defied all laws of gravity by falling from its place on the shelf above the washing machine to inside it. Not only was the stainless steel drum now dripping with honey, it was also crawling with delirious, satiated bees that had flown from their nest outside the window and into the washing machine too.

It was now my extra job in the family (we all had jobs on Saturdays) to scrape the bees and honey off the drum with a teaspoon and dispose of the corpses. While I was on my hands and knees, head stuck inside the washing machine, it occurred to me that this was how suicidal women poets ended their life, except they stuck their head into a gas oven. There was something humiliating and religious about kneeling down to remove the bees but I couldn't summon the energy to work out why because I was in too much pain. At least five of the bees had somehow gathered up enough energy before dying to sting my hand and no one was particularly sympathetic. My mother said, 'Yes, bees do sting,' and told me to put my hand under cold water. As an afterthought, she said, 'In Russia they actually rub bees' venom onto arthritic joints.' I tried to bribe my younger brother Sam to do the job for me, but he was too busy blow-drying his hair into a teddy boy quiff. 'Bees have lots of eyes,' he shouted over the whir of Mom's hair dryer, 'about six each.' We had both seen a programme on the telly where they showed a close-up of a bee that was apparently a 'keystone mutualist' because it pollinated seed-laden fruits in desert communities. The voice-over said that honey bees were the highest form of insect life and that a strong colony flies the equivalent distance to the moon every day. Then they showed men in a field smoking the bees out of a hive. What was I supposed to do? Set fire to the washing machine? Desperate to get out of my life as fast as possible, I tried putting four jasmine joss sticks into the holes of the steel drum and lighting them. I reckoned the smoke would make the keystone mutualists fly out on their own accord without having to scoop them up into my teaspoon. But I knew they were the highest form of insect life and couldn't be bothered to move. All that happened was ash fell from the joss sticks into the honey and I had to clear burnt-up sticks and ash as well as the bees who obviously thought they were in heaven. I didn't blame them for not wanting to budge because I could see from their point of view that a washing machine full of honey was more appealing than the grey suburb I was wasting my life in – a desert community without the bonus of sunshine or seed laden fruits.

By ten o'clock, when the last four of the plump, drunk and hedonistic bees had been wrapped in the sports page of *The Times* and dumped in the bin, I grabbed my black straw hat and waved goodbye to my mother so she could see my swollen fingers and suffer immense remorse.

'You've got to clean the oven. That's your second job.'

I tried to stare at her blankly but my eyes began to hurt. The effort it took to look cool and unfazed by everything was exhausting me. I walked down the stairs tripping over my denim flares, banged the front door with my smarting right hand which was hot and red from the stings and attempted to run in my new lime green platform shoes. As I passed the Chinese take away called HOLY and the dry cleaners called REUBANS, a pensioner dragging her beige plastic trolley in zigzags across the pavement said, 'I like your funny hat.'

It was very very urgent that I got out of my life.

Inside the greasy spoon's steamed up windows and haze of cigarette smoke, this sense of urgency accelerated. I had so little time. Time for what? I didn't know but I was convinced there was another sort of life waiting for me and I had to work out what it was before I cleaned the oven. I hastily ordered eggs, beans, bacon and bubble and squeak, and then, realizing I didn't have enough money for beans and bubble and squeak, decided to cancel the beans. Holding a mug of scalding tea in my unstung hand, I made my way past the builders and bus drivers towards a Formica table to begin my impersonation of the writer's life. As soon as I sat down I reached for the white paper napkins that were kept in a glass alongside the salt, pepper, ketchup and brown sauce and started to write with a leaking blue biro. This is the word I wrote on my napkin:

ENGLAND

'England' was an exciting word to write. My mother had told me we were in exile and would one day return to the country of my birth. The idea that I was living in Exile and not in England terrified me. When I told my new friend Judy (who was born in Lewisham) that I didn't really want to live in Exile, she said, 'Yeah, I'd be scared shitless too.' Judy wanted to look like Liza Minnelli in the film *Cabaret* and Liza was American. Judy's father was a docker and he was as English as they come. He had died of cancer, something to do with asbestos in the cargo he landed, but Judy didn't really know the whole story. On the weekends I painted her fingernails with sparkling green nail varnish to turn her in to Liza so she wouldn't always have to be Judy whose father had died in England when she was twelve years old.

There were certain things about England that I still couldn't quite grasp. One of these ungraspable things occurred right here in the café. The greasy spoon cook who was called Angie always gave me bacon that I considered raw. It was as if she put it on the hot plate to make it warm but not to actually cook it. This was very upsetting to me because the livid pink rasher on my plate made me think of the pig it had been sliced off. Somewhere in England there was a pig that was still alive running around with a chunk sliced off its side. I did not feel I could ask Angie to cook the bacon for longer because I did not live in England – I lived in Exile – and reckoned this was the way things were done in the country that was my host.

'I can't fall apart because I've never fallen together.'

This was something my teenage hero had written, or words that meant something like that – the man whose blank stare I practised in front of the mirror. I reckoned that every time Andy Warhola painted a tin of American soup it was his way of escaping from the flat brown fields of Eastern Europe where his parents were born. Every single tin of clam chowder got him nearer New York and away from living in Exile with his mother in Pittsburgh. Andy's words were like a prayer I said every night before I went to sleep, and they rolled around my mind now as I sat in the greasy spoon piling up napkins to write England on. While I drank my mug of tea and watched the red London buses arrive and depart from the station, I thought about his collection of wigs. Apparently he stored them in boxes in his factory in New York and actually glued them to his head. I was interested in Andy because I reckoned I was a bit in disguise too. Judy wasn't really in disguise as Liza (she wore velvet hot pants and fishnet tights to the Wimpy). Everyone could see what she was aiming for because they had seen *Cabaret* too, but I was not really sure what I was aiming for, especially as Andy was a man. She told me to focus on David Bowie, the star man who came from Beckenham, which was quite near Lewisham, but who now lived in exile on the planet Mars.

English people were kind. They called me pet and love and said sorry when I bumped into them. I was clumsy because I was sleepwalking through England and English people didn't mind because they were sleep walking through England too. I reckoned this was because it got dark so early in winter. It was as if someone pulled the plug out of England at 4pm. Most curiously of all, when Joan next door tied her dog to the Wall's ice cream stand outside the corner shop she spoke to her pet as if it could talk back.

'Holly, say hello to the girl.'

There was always an embarrassing silence after she said that. But Joan wasn't embarrassed. Even if her dog just scratched its ear or gazed at the chewing gum stuck on the pavement, she always had an excuse for why Holly didn't actually talk. 'Oh she's in a funny mood today isn't she?'

EnglAND
eNGLAND
ENgland

As well as the England doodles I also wrote sentences very fast on the white paper napkins. This action (scribbling) and also my costume (the black straw hat) were like being armed with an AK-47: the sort of rifle the newspapers always show third-world children holding instead of an ice cream with a flake bar stuck in the middle of it. As far as the builders sitting next to me were concerned, I was not quite there. I had written myself in to some other kind of status and they didn't feel easy about chatting me up or asking me to pass the salt. I was out of it.

Writing made me feel wiser than I actually was. Wise and sad. That was what I thought writers should be. I was sad anyway, much sadder than the sentences I wrote. I was a sad girl impersonating a sad girl. My mother and father had just separated. Some of Dad's clothes were still in the cupboard (jacket, shoes, a hanger full of ties) but his books had disappeared from the shelves. Worst of all, he had left his forlorn shaving brush and box of migraine tablets in the bath room cabinet. Love between Mom and Dad had gone wrong in England. Sam knew and I knew but there was nothing we could do about it. When love goes wrong, instead of seeing the front of things we saw the backs of things. Our parents always walking away from each other. Making a separate lonely space even when they sat together at the family table. Both of them staring into the middle distance. When love goes wrong everything goes wrong. Wrong enough for my father to knock on my bedroom door and tell me he was going to live somewhere else. He was wearing his English suit and he looked torn up, like the road outside.

When Angie carried the English breakfast to my table, she hovered too near me and for too long, pretending to re-arrange the bottle of brown sauce. I knew she wanted to ask me where I was from because she could see I was curious about things that were quite normal to her. The red double-decker buses. The men smoking Number 6 after they tucked into the pile of beans and chips on their plate. The fact I asked for tomato sauce and not ketchup or said robot instead of traffic lights and thenk yoo instead of thank you. Angie had given me a portion of beans even though I had cancelled them. English people were so kind it was unbelievable. I loved my new country and wanted to belong to it and be as English as Angie, though it occurred to me she might not be entirely English because I had heard her talking in Italian to the man who owned the greasy spoon.

I was so pleased about the extra beans. I pierced one of them with my fork while I doodled on the napkins. The prospect of returning home to the house which no longer had Dad in it was unbearable.

I counted the beans on my plate. Thankfully there were about twenty of them, so that would give me a bit of time to work out how I was going to get to my other life. The existential writers who I thought might give me some clues – I always got the letters of Jean Paul Sartre's last name mixed up so it came out as Jean Paul Stare – probably didn't have to clean ovens with evil Brillo pads.

They were evil because they were not just squares of scratchy material with pink detergent stuck to a piece of felt on the end. As far as I was concerned, they had been designed to waste the lives of girls and women. This thought made me so desperate that I ordered a slice of extra toast to slow the injustice of things down. Jean Paul Stare was French. Andy Warhol was half Czech but totally American and so was Liza Minnelli, who like Angie might be half Italian and all the rest of it. I wrote down some of the rest of it on the napkins with my leaky biro and it took quite a long time. When I looked up all the bus drivers and builders had gone back to work and Angie was asking me to pay for my extra toast. I hadn't even noticed she had brought it to the table and I still had fifteen beans to get through. Worst of all, she was blatantly staring at the napkins I held in my right hand, the word ENGLAND biro'd into all of them.

'Shall I hold those for you?'

I didn't want Angie to hold my napkins because

they were part of my secret life and they were also going to be my first novel even though they only had England biro'd into them and a few odd words and phrases. She watched me search for coins in my purse, all the while clutching onto the napkins as if something terrible would happen to me if I let go of them. Three of her teeth were completely rotten, the colour of the steaming teabags she scooped out of the urn with a spoon.

'What did you do to your hand?'

'I got stung by some bees.'

Angie screwed up her nose in sympathy and made her lips mime ouch, which was more than my mother had done.

'Where were the bees then?'

'They were in the washing machine.'

'Ah.' This time she rolled her eyes towards the nicotine-stained ceiling.

'A pot of honey fell into the washing machine and the bees from outside flew in.'

'Right.' She smiled. And then she asked the question I knew she wanted to ask ever since I walked into the greasy spoon.

'Where are you from?'

Now that I was fifteen years old, South Africa was the part of my life I tried not to think about. Every new day in England was an opportunity to practise being happy and to teach my new friends how to swim. I reckoned that if the council filled the pool with tea, everyone in England would be happy to put their heads under water. They would soon all become champion swimmers and win gold medals a go-go.

'Where are you from then?'

Angie repeated her question in case I hadn't understood it the first time.

'I don't know.'

'Well you don't know much do you?'

I decided it was best to agree with her.

As I left the greasy spoon with the England napkins in my hands, I was cold and knew the central heating at home wasn't working. Two days ago, the man who came to fix it said: 'I officially condemn this boiler. The law says you've got to buy a new one,' and then he winked and switched it on again and told us to give him a ring if it played up again – which it did, two hours after he left the house where Mom had made him a cup of tea in a mug that had the word 'Amandla!' written on it. Mom said, 'Amandla is a Zulu word, it means POWER.' The heating man said, 'Well you should have a bit of power in your boiler for a few years yet.'

By the time I got to the Chinese take-away called HOLY, I pressed my cheek against the window and waited for my life to change. A large bag of bean sprouts was propped up outside the take-away which had a sign on the door that said it was closed.

A Chinese girl, also about fifteen, opened the

front door and hoiked the bag of bean sprouts up from the pavement.

'We're not open till six o'clock,' she shouted.

I stared at her jeans which had home-made flares stitched into the denim. Her 'I Love NY' T-shirt came to just above her belly button and she wore white stiletto shoes. She stared at my black straw hat and then lowered her eyes to take in the lime green platform shoes I was so proud of and which I believed would help me escape from Finchley, even if for the time being they just gave me a different view of things. A woman's voice was calling to her, shouting out some orders. Like me she was a girl who had jobs to do.

When I arrived home (West Finchley), I was in despair. How was I ever going to escape from living in exile? I wanted to be in exile from exile. To make matters worse, Sam was now lying on the sofa in the living room thrashing a drum he'd wedged between his knees. When he saw me, he stopped drumming for three seconds and started to say profound things.

'You know how chicken legs are called drum sticks?'

'Yeah?'

'Hhhhaa hhhhaa Hhhhha Hhhhhhaa.'

He was such a maniac. I started to laugh too. And then he told me to shut up because our au pair was in the next room and he was in a 'mood'.

Two months after Dad left our first proper English house in West Finchley, our mother said she was going to get an au pair to 'hold the fort' while she was at work. Sam and I were expecting a pretty young woman from Sweden with a blonde pony tail. Instead, when our au pair arrived on the doorstep, he was carrying a huge book called *The Sixth Plenary Session of the Sixth Central Committee of the Communist Party of China 1938*. He was balding, pot-bellied, bad tempered, and explained his name was 'Farid with an F'. We couldn't work out why he bothered to tell us about the F and he didn't even ask us our names, he just gave us orders. Farid told us he was writing his PhD and we were required to run him a bath regularly, also that he liked his tea with a slice of lemon and three sugars. He was so appalled by the standard of hygiene in our home that when he came back from the London School of Economics he shut himself up in his room and guzzled three bags of pistachio nuts rather than cook in our kitchen. Farid couldn't understand why nothing in the kitchen had a lid on it. We didn't understand either. Even the brand new pot of yoghurt, completely untouched because the silver foil was still unbroken, was now standing by the sink without a lid. Someone in the family has just ripped it off for the sake of it. The one time Farid cleaned the kitchen floor, he squashed a wet towel under his bare feet and walked across the lino scrunching his toes in disgust at the chicken bones and tops of ketchup bottles, yelling something about how his mother in Cairo would never have let her house get into this kind of mess.

We secretly agreed with Farid and wished we could all go and live in Cairo too. Yeah, we would shut ourselves up in our nice clean rooms and throw away the key and look out of the window at the pyramids and wait for someone to bring us sandwiches – which is what we did for Farid – who regularly told us he didn't like peanut butter because it sat in his stomach like a bullet. But today, Saturday, our new au pair was beside himself. When Sam began drumming again, Farid marched in to the living room, furious, fat and shaking.

Did we not understand he was trying to WRITE in his bedroom? Did we not understand he had to finish his dissertation on Karl Marx by Monday morning? Did we not know the meaning of the word PhD, how it would put food into his little daughter's mouth and send her to a good school? Our au pair had gone bright red and he was sweating. All around him were posters on the wall of black South African women marching against the pass laws – 'YOU HAVE STRUCK WOMEN YOU HAVE STRUCK A ROCK' splashed across the centre in angry capital letters. Next to it was an oil painting of an African woman with a box on her head walking barefoot alongside a man on a bicycle, two figures walking into dust and sky. On the kilim rug were three lids that had been thrown haphazardly onto the rug. Ketchup, Marmite, Branston Pickle.

'WHY DON'T YOU KEEDS (Farid always said keeds instead of kids) EVER PUT THE LID BACK ON?'

He was on to something. Although we never talked about it, the whole lid thing was something of a mystery to us all. We secretly wanted to live in a house where everything had a lid on it. Not a day went past without one of us staring forlornly at yet another bottle or jar that now stood lidless on the shelves. We never asked each other to put the lid back on because we suspected we might be incapable of doing this ourselves. It was possible that leaving the lids off happened after Dad left the house, but we really couldn't remember and didn't want to think about it anyway. While Sam drummed wildly, his shiny eyes fixed on the wall opposite the sofa, I asked Farid if he knew where our mother was? Farid always knew where Mom was because she was his bread and butter. In fact, she was so nice to Farid we had started to resent him. 'Your poor mother,' Farid snarled, 'has gone shopping.'

'SHOPP-ING SHOPP-ING SHOPP-ING,' Sam chanted over and over again, laughing and drumming at the same time. Farid lunged at Sam and snatched the drum out of his hands. And then he grabbed the bamboo stick as well and started to beat Sam's leg with it. Above his head was a world peace poster showing three children playing happily in a field with a ball, a yoyo and a badminton racket. Farid was now out of control. He bent his fat knees so that he could strike harder. Sometimes he missed Sam and hit the wall instead.

'DO YOU NOT UNDERSTAND WHAT IT IS LIKE TO BE A STRANGER IN YOUR COUNTRY?'

Farid saying that made me laugh hysterically while Sam howled.

'YOU KEEEDS' – whack whack – 'DO YOU NOT UNDERSTAND' – whack – 'THAT I AM NOT FROM YOUR COUNTRY?'

The top button of his shirt had popped off and sweat dripped down his cheeks.

'I DO NOT HAVE EVEN ONE PAIR OF SHOES THAT ARE RIGHT FOR THIS WET COLD PLACE.'

That's what happened to us too. When we first arrived in England we never had the right clothes. In January we wore duffle coats and flip flops. February was the month of wellingtons and a sleeveless polka-dot dress. And June, which was supposed to be the beginning of summer, was the month we all finally got it together and wore thermal vests, boots, gloves and thick woollen hats.

I liked it that Farid had said, 'Your country'. Yes, I said to myself, I am English. As English as they come. While Farid tried to beat my brother, I looked at the curtains my father had hemmed in blanket stitch one night after work. He had made them a week before he left the family house. Sam and I had stood on either side of him, leaning in to see his big fingers holding the tiny silver needle. When Sam tied a knot in the cotton thread and handed it back, Dad had said: 'I think we are getting to know each other again aren't we?'

Farid was nothing like our Dad. For a start, had our father still lived at home, he would have said, 'Don't torture the oven. Smooth the Brillo pad gently over the surface.' Why did he always say don't torture the kettle, don't torture the light switch, don't torture the ice cubes? My father had a very intimate relationship with objects like kettles and door handles and keys. According to him they had to be understood, never bullied or tortured. To fill a kettle through its snout and not to take the lid off was to humiliate the kettle. To turn a door handle too roughly was to 'duff it up'. He would not tolerate what he called 'brutality' to inanimate objects.

While Farid and my brother rolled on the floor punching each other, I could hear people mowing their lawns and washing their cars, the sort of things that happened in England on Saturdays, while Joan next door shouted to her dog, 'HOLLY HOLLY HOLLY come home for your tea.'

Farid had somehow managed to get up onto his feet and was staring at Sam's face.

'Som,' he said.

Farid seemed to want to say something else but couldn't get the words out. Still staring at my brother, he eventually asked where our father actually was? Why was it that he was not living with us in the family house?

'Mom and Dad have separated.'

Farid shook his head, puzzled. For the first time since he arrived on our door step it occurred to me he might be a kind man. He even started to collect up the lids from the floor.

When Mom got back with the shopping, she said, 'Everything is very calm. How nice to come back to children who are not fighting with each other for a change.' She lifted up a bottle of Asti Spumante from the shopping bags and slipped it in to the fridge along with six pots of hazelnut yogurt. Good, I thought. I'll take that fizzy wine out of the fridge when it's cold and I'll run with it to the park. Then I'll drink it all and jump under a moving car, leaving my napkins with ENGLAND biro'd on them to my biographers. They will flock to the house in Finchley to see where I lived and a blue plaque will be nailed on to the bricks and mortar of our first English house. As usual my brother took it upon himself to interrupt my thoughts and stir things up.

'Farid hit me,' Sam whined to Mom.

'Did you Farid?'

'Yes, I did,' Farid confessed in a meek, pathetic voice.

'He was banging the drum while I was translating Marx's essay on wage labour written for the German Working-Man's Club in Brussels.'

'Farid,' Mom said sternly, 'Never hit my children again or you'll be out on your ear.'

Our au pair smiled. He looked happy for the first time since he arrived.

That night, we ordered an Indian take-away and watched *Steptoe and Son* on the television. Sam lay with his head in Mom's lap and begged to be spoon-fed dhal like a pasha. Farid sat in the armchair Dad had always sat in but we didn't mind anymore. He said he had a stomach ache from all the stress yet managed to finish his own lamb madras and polish off my chicken korma as well.

'I like this family very much. You are good people even though you do not know how to make a home. But I have no home in England so I am honoured you have given me a room in your tent.'

By the time I got to bed, I felt weird and shaky. I had lived in England for six years and was nearly as English as they come. All the same I had come from somewhere else. I missed the smell of plants I could not name, the sound of birds I could not name, the murmur of languages I could not name. Where exactly was Southern Africa? One day I would look at a map and find out. That night I lay awake all night long. I had so many questions to ask the world from my bedroom in West Finchley about the country I was born in. How do people become cruel and depraved? If you torture someone, are you mad or are you normal? If a white man sets his dog on a black child and everyone says that's okay, if the neighbours and police and judges and teachers say, 'That's fine by me,' is life worth living? What about the people who don't think it's okay? Are there enough of them in the world?

As the milkman clanked down milk bottles on our door step, I suddenly knew why the lids for honey and ketchup and peanut butter were never in their right place in our family house. The lids, like us, did not have a place. I was born in one country and grew up in another, but I was not sure which one I belonged to. And another thing. I did not want to know this thing, but I did know all the same. Putting a lid on was like pretending our mother and father were back together again, attached to each other instead of prised apart.

I rolled off the bed and found the napkins I had saved from the greasy spoon. I saw the word 'England' biro'd into the tissue, crumpled and stained with bacon fat, but I couldn't work out what I was trying to say. I knew I wanted to be a writer more than anything else in the world, but I was overwhelmed by everything and didn't know where to start.

Four

– Aesthetic Enthusiasm –

I t is sometimes necessary to know where to stop.' The Chinese shopkeeper had probably noticed that my hand was resting quite close to his shirt cuff when he said that. The palm trees outside the restaurant were covered in snow by the time we had finished our bottle of wine. In fact, the tracks and paths that mapped the way back to my hotel had more or less disappeared. He still had not told me his name. I had not told him mine either, although I knew he knew it because he'd read one of my books. For some reason, knowing each other's names was something we did not want to know. He leaned over towards the German couple at the table nearby and congratulated them for having had the foresight to bring arctic clothing to Majorca in spring. 'My friend here,' he pointed to me, 'is dressed for the beach'.

The German man began to tell us, in English, how they had encountered a snake on a hike in the mountains earlier that morning. It was lucky they were wearing boots. The snake was hiding in a crack in a rock. It might even have been a rattlesnake. Did we know that dead snakes can bite for up to an hour after their death?

'Yes,' the Chinese shopkeeper said, 'I did know that.' He turned to me and began to talk about soup again. He was obsessed with soup. Apparently, although he'd forgotten how to make one sort of Chinese soup, he still remembered how to make another sort. It was more like rice porridge than soup, very nourishing and warming in winter, and he liked to add sesame oil and pepper to it. I couldn't help noticing that his hand was now resting quite close to my hand, and he might have noticed too, because of what he said next.

'Now tell me, where do you think your skin is thinnest on the body?'

'On the finger tips?'

'No. I'll tell you now. It is thinnest on the eyelids and it is thickest on the palms and soles.'

I laughed and he smiled. Then he laughed and I smiled. He said he missed the smell of roasted peanuts in China and he'd forgotten how to make the seafood kind of Chinese soup, but, he was very pleased he'd made a new life in the mountains of Majorca because that is where I had invited him to join me at my table for three. And then he nudged me because Maria had just walked in to the restaurant and was stamping the snow off her boots. She looked surprisingly tall in a heavy coat trimmed with fur. I waved to her and she made her way to our table. Maria was carrying a small suitcase in her gloved hand. Her face was stern and sad.

'My brother told me you were cold in your room.'

'Yes.'

'I have moved you to another room. There are blankets on your bed.'

'Thank you.'

'Are you going somewhere Maria?'

'Yes.'

Maria did not want to talk. Not at all.

I opened my bag and gave her the chocolate I had bought at the Chinese shopkeeper's shop, 'intensidad', with the big 99% on it. And then I counted out the rent for my hotel room, four nights in cash, because I thought she might need it for whatever she had to do next. She was pleased to take the cash. When she kissed my cheek I could feel her heart beating under her coat, fierce and roaring.

Later, when the Chinese shopkeeper walked me up the invisible mountain path to the hotel, he said again, 'Sometimes in life, it's not about knowing where to start, it's knowing where to stop.' He told me that when he was living in Paris all those years ago, he was lonely at the weekends, so he decided to take the train to Marseilles. He was walking near the port and the mistral was blowing and he hardly spoke any French, but when he saw two cops stop a North African boy, probably no more than ten years old, he stopped too. The boy was wearing a childish white cotton vest. It probably smelt of the soap powder his mother had washed it in. The cops lifted up his vest and started to punch his stomach. That was something he could not forget, the sight of adult men lifting up the vest of a child so as to hurt him more accurately. He found himself walking over to the boy who was tough and taking the punches, and he shouted to the cops in his funny Chinese French accent, 'Stop, stop, stop, stop, stop.' It was not exactly heroic but it was what he wanted them to do. They did stop. They stopped and walked away.

The Chinese shopkeeper said, 'You will want to stop here because we have arrived at your hotel.' We stopped by the terrace and his head moved closer to mine. I could see the silver in his black hair.

When we kissed, I knew we were both in the middle of some sort of catastrophe and I didn't know if something was starting or if it was stopping. The collar of his big winter coat was wet where the snow was melting. He took off his coat and handed it to me. 'If you go for a walk you will need it and I have another one. You need to dress properly for the weather you find yourself in.'

After a while, I walked up the marble stairs, past the large cactus that stood in a pot on the landing and up to the battered oak door of a room on the second floor. I opened the door with the key Maria had slipped in to my hand when I gave her the cash. It was smaller than my room upstairs. Folded neatly on the end of the bed were a pile of blankets, and

106

placed in front of a window that looked out on to the ancient palm tree in the garden was a desk and chair. It had obviously been tricky to squeeze the desk in, but Maria had carried it through the door and pushed it between the window and the bed.

I had a view. I had a writing desk. The room was warm. Burning in the fire were three large logs. In a basket nearby were other logs stacked neatly on top of each other. The room was so warm I knew the logs had been burning for some time.

Maria had left in a rush. In a snowstorm. Had she outgrown this world she'd made up here in the mountains? Was she not looking forward to picking the lemons and oranges in the orchard she had irrigated? She had also planted the vegetables and olive trees and built the beehives from which she gathered the thick, aromatic honey she served at breakfast. It was Maria who baked the bread and ground the coffee beans. The logs that would keep me warm through the night were chopped by her too. Maria had left in a rage and without enough cash. Did she want to stride out on her own and get on with whatever it is she had to do next?

It occurred to me that both Maria and I were on the run in the twenty-first century, just like George Sand whose name was also Amantine was on the run in the nineteenth century, and Maria whose name was also Zama was looking for somewhere to recover and rest in the twentieth. We were on the run from the lies concealed in the language of politics, from myths about our character and our purpose in life. We were on the run from our own desires too probably, whatever they were. It was best to laugh it off.

The way we laugh. At our own desires. The way we mock ourselves. Before anyone else can. The way we are wired to kill. Ourselves. It doesn't bear thinking about.

There was something else I did not want to think about. That afternoon, when I stood by the sea and laughed at myself under the snow clouds, what had come to mind was the piano in Maria's hallway, the piano that was polished every day but never played. I did not want to know that I had been shut down like that piano. For some reason I remembered the way I used to eat oranges as a child in Johannesburg. First I had to find one that would fit into the palm of my hand. So I searched the sack in the pantry for a small orange because the small ones were the juiciest. Then I rolled the orange under my bare foot to make it soft. It took a long time and the point was to get the fruit to yield its juice and not to split. This had to be sensed entirely through the sole of the foot. My legs were brown and strong. I felt so powerful when I figured out how to use my strength on something as small as an orange. When it was ready I made a hole in the peel with my thumb and sucked out the sweet juice. This strange memory in turn reminded me of a line from a poem by Apollinaire. I had written down this line in the Polish notebook, twenty years ago: 'The window opens like an orange.'

The mute piano and the window opening like an orange and the Polish notebook I had brought to Majorca with me were connected to my unpublished novel, *Swimming Home*. I realised that the question I had asked myself while writing this book was (as surgeons say) very close to the bone: 'What do we do with knowledge that we cannot bear to live with? What do we do with the things we do not want to know?'

I did not know how to get the work, my writing, into the world. I did not know how to open the window like an orange. If anything, the window had closed like an axe on my tongue. If this was to be my reality, I did not know what to do with it.

As I watched the snow gather on the fronds of the palm tree in Maria's garden, I asked myself another question. Should I accept my lot? If I was to buy a ticket and travel all the way to acceptance, if I was to greet it and shake its hand, if I was to entwine my fingers with acceptance and walk hand in hand with acceptance every day, what would that feel like? After a while I realised I could not accept my question. A female writer cannot afford to feel her life too clearly. If she does, she will write in a rage when she should write calmly.

She will write in a rage when she should write calmly. She will write foolishly where she should write wisely. She will write of herself where she should write of her characters. She is at war with her lot.

– *A Room of One's Own*, Virginia Woolf (1929)

I had told the Chinese shop keeper that to become a writer, I had to learn to interrupt, to speak up, to speak a little louder, and then louder, and then to just speak in my own voice which is not loud at all. My conversation with him had taken me to places I did not want to revisit. I had not expected to return to Africa while sheltering from a snowstorm in Majorca. Yet, as he had pointed out, Africa had already returned to me when I found myself sobbing on escalators in London. If I thought I was not thinking about the past, the past was thinking about me. I reckoned this was true because the Chinese shopkeeper, whose father was a steel worker, had told me that escalators, or the 'revolving staircase' patented in 1859 by Nathan Ames of Massachusetts and then re-designed by the engineer Jesse Reno, were first described to the modern world as an 'endless conveyor'.

I rearranged the chair and sat at the desk. And then I looked at the walls to check out the power points so I could plug in my laptop. The hole in the wall nearest to the desk was placed above the basin, a precarious socket for a gentleman's electric razor.

That spring in Majorca, when life was very hard and I simply could not see where there was to get to, it occurred to me that where I had to get to was that socket. Even more useful to a writer than a room of her own is an extension lead and a variety of adaptors for Europe, Asia and Africa.

Deborah Levy's note: The line: 'I simply couldn't see where there was to get to' references Sylvia Plath's poem 'The Moon and the Yew Tree'.

A NOTE ON THE AUTHOR

Deborah Levy writes fiction, plays, and poetry. Her work has been staged by the Royal Shakespeare Company and widely broadcast on the BBC, including her dramatizations of two of Freud's most iconic case histories, *Dora* and *The Wolfman*. The author of highly praised novels including the Man Booker Prize–shortlisted *Swimming Home*, *Beautiful Mutants*, *Swallowing Geography*, and *Billy and Girl*, she lives in London.